The Globe
Challenge

The Globe Challenge

Highlights from The Globe and Mail's
weekly contest of wit and word play

Warren Clements, editor

GLOBE AND MAIL PUBLISHING

The Globe Challenge
Copyright © 1993 by Globe and Mail Publishing

Publisher: Michael J. Ryan

First published in 1993 by
Globe and Mail Publishing
A division of Globe Information Services
444 Front Street West
Toronto, Ontario
M5V 2S9
(416) 585-5250
Fax: (416) 585-5249

ISBN: 0-921925-52-2

Cover design and illustration: Thomas Dannenberg

Cartoons: Warren Clements

Printed and bound in Canada by Metropole Litho Inc.

Foreword

The Challenge first saw daylight in February, 1991.
  Since then, Saturday after Saturday, some of the wittiest amateur (and occasionally professional) writers in
  the country have competed for space, scribbling their
  entries on yellow scrap paper, typing them on cream-coloured bond with elegant letterheads, or faxing
  them from businesses, law firms or the local copy
  shop.
My job as editor is to let in as many gems as the column
  can accommodate and to close the door, with regret,
  on the others. This book touches many of the high
  spots to date, and includes a few ingenious entries
  that didn't fit the first time around.
All entries are credited to their authors. Where several
  items are by the same author, the name appears at the
  end of the list. Many names crop up regularly, and
  one of the regulars, Alanna Little, offered "some observations from this side of the Challenge desk" in a
  letter she wrote after the hundredth Challenge appeared in May, 1993:
"Most of the comments I receive from people who notice my entries are positive, even flattering. But occasionally they're in the vein: 'Who helped you with
  that?' To which the only answer is: 'Glad you like it.
  Who explained it to you?'
"Sometimes people have told me that they often do the
  Challenge but don't send it in. Which is probably
  true, as it does take a fair bit of courage — especially
  some entries, eh, Mr. Clements. Then there are those
  who would do it if they weren't too busy (implication: with more important things), and of course
  theirs would be really something!

"Then there's the Challenge Law. Once the Canada Post pigeon has taken my envelope I discover (a) a ghastly typo, (b) my clever entries in fact are utterly banal, (c) both, (d) I think of something else, this time remarkably witty."

As an incentive to get the column started, I promised a copy of The Globe and Mail Style Book to the weekly winner, and that became the standard prize. Choosing those winners has itself been a challenge; I have often turned to colleague Brian Gable for a second opinion, and have appreciated his valuable advice. (But if you didn't win, blame me, not him.)

My thanks to Joan Danard, Sarah Murdoch and Colin Haskin of The Globe's weekend Focus section, where The Challenge appears, for their wise counsel and editing of the weekly column. Josée Gauthier of Globe Information Services was instrumental in getting this book off the ground; Alan Husdal and Kathryn O'Handley designed it, and Thomas Dannenberg created the cover; kudos to all. And my love to Sandra, who has learned not to expect me home until late on Tuesday nights.

Above all, heartfelt thanks to the authors of this book, the legions of Globe readers who said to themselves, "I wonder if I can do that," and have done so as though born to it. To the many contributors without whom this book would not exist, and who were aptly described in one of the column's headlines as the Challengentsia: a toast!

Define a Canadian

The challenge was to define a Canadian. The idea came from Joan Danard, inspired by writer Rich Marin's line that a Canadian is someone who says "thank you" to a bank machine. Christopher Gudgeon sent in a page of similar items he had written for Geist magazine, a few of which appear below.

A Canadian is someone who...:

On seeing a light at the end of the tunnel, assumes it
    is a train.
When given a compliment, always looks behind to
    see for whom it is intended.   *R. W. Crosby*

Knows the difference between the Northern Lights
    and a Northern Lite.   *Victoria Napier*

Scoffs at patriotic exhibitionism by Americans while
lamenting the lack of spirit shown on his own
national days.
Knows how to count his blessings but doesn't add
them up in public.
Thinks an income-tax refund is a gift from the
government.
Believes anyone who knows the words to *O Canada* is
either an immigrant or a zealot.   *Edward W. Barrett*

Doesn't know anyone who owns a flag.
Wears shorts in March, apologizes to panhandlers,
goes to the back of a line, feels sorry for Wayne
Gretzky and finds Kentucky Fried Chicken "a bit
too spicy."   *David Linklater*

Holds the world record for telephone use, probably
listening to: "Don't hang up. Your call is important
to us..."   *Ken Purvis*

Is constantly pulling himself/herself up by the roots
to see whether he/she is still growing.

Robert C. Hamilton

Will drive to an unemployment protest meeting in his
  Toyota.   *Al Lever*

Thinks he speaks English without an accent.
Saves her cents-off coupons and drives all over town
  to redeem them.
Carefully weighs both sides of an issue before
  decisively calling for further study.
Loves Canadian theatre once it's a hit on Broadway.
                                               Alanna Little

Is able to say "Progressive Conservative" and
  "Ministry of Culture" without laughing.
Is a true patriot who wonders when the people of the
  other provinces will learn to be less selfish.
Is sure that CPR works only on board a train.
Is fond of boasting that he is more modest than an
  American.
Is willing to subsidize CBC programming provided he
  doesn't have to watch it.
Is disgusted by all the complaining going on, and isn't
  afraid to say so.
Is convinced that democracy involves keeping your
  opinions to yourself.   *Al Wilkinson*

In a restaurant, apologizes for not being ready to
  order at the waiter's convenience.   *Ian D. Brown*

Spends a lot of time trying to figure out what a
  Canadian is.
Regardless of service, always leaves a tip in a
  restaurant.   *Ruth Brown*

Resents being called an American by foreigners, and
a foreigner by Americans.
Will travel across the border to buy cigarettes and
return home for subsidized cancer therapy.

Alexandre Menard

Crosses the road to get to the middle. *Trevor Wickham*

Is late for his appointment because he is busy leaving
a note on the car illegally parked in the
"handicapped" zone.
Says "sorry" when you accidentally bump into him.

Eusebio L. Koh

Waits for the light to change before crossing a
deserted intersection at 3 a.m. *Robert Davis*

Takes as a signal for a standing ovation any two
people who happen to be leaving during curtain
calls.
Writes a cheque to support live theatre in Canada
while watching a rerun of *I Love Lucy*.
Believes the Free Trade Agreement is an agreement
about free trade. *Jim Parr*

Flies from Toronto to Vancouver to attend a Save Via
Rail rally. *K.C. Angus*

Says "no big deal" to a sidewalk cyclist who has just
knocked him down. *Eric Adams*

Prefers an inoffensive rodent to an aggressive bird of
prey. *R.M. Baxter*

Knows lots about U.S. television awards shows, but
thinks Gemini belongs only in a horoscope.
Grumbles about Indians' tax-free status while
cheerfully buying gas or cigarettes on the nearest
reserve. *Mary Dando*

Would enter a contest to win a Globe and Mail Style
Book. *Lorraine Oake*

Considers turning up the thermostat an integral part
of foreplay. *Carolyn Germain Smith*

Says "excuse me" when he burps, even if he's all
alone. *Georgina L. Clark*

On arriving at an airport in a foreign country and
without having any goods to declare, avoids using
the green exit because of vague feelings of guilt,
and instead uses the red exit in order to assure the
customs officials that he or she indeed has nothing
to declare. *Glen Acorn*

Feels no pressure to know a lot about wine.
Goes to hot-tub parties where people wear bathing
suits.
Finds himself thinking about sending off to
Hinterland Who's Who for "further information on
the loon."
Lies in bed at night wondering what Casey and
Finnegan are really like.
Feels deep down inside that he has this innate ability
to use snowshoes. *Christopher Gudgeon*

Says hello to anyone walking a dog.
Says "no thanks" to a telemarketing tape.
Never sits in someone else's seat, even if the
 ticket-holder doesn't show.   *Marg Gillies*

Carries travellers cheques in a moneybelt.
                                    Dwayne W. Rowe

Heartily proclaims, "Sure it's 38 below, but it's a dry
 cold."
Believes that true bilingualism will be achieved only
 when one faucet indicates "C" for Cold and the
 other indicates "C" for Chaud.
Believes a royal commission should be appointed to
 determine whether twist-ties should be turned
 clockwise or counterclockwise.   *Mariam Bernstein*

When he musters enough courage to buy a Rolex
 watch, wears it hidden under a long-sleeve shirt
 and an Eaton's suit.   *Byron Bellows*

Tries to work Canada Day so he can take the
 following Friday off.   *Procter LeMare*

Unlikely Remarks

The challenge was to submit statements you will probably never hear. The idea came from Sander Schimmelpenninck, whose examples included: "You are not the first customer to complain about our service."

"Oh, if I've interrupted your dinner I can hang up right now. And if you're really not interested in what we're selling, how about if I don't even bother calling back?"

"I didn't think labour was that bad. And I kind of liked childbirth. It was kind of fun."   *M. Storey*

"Can you speak up, Ms. Copps? I can't hear you."

"Senator Kennedy would love another club soda."

"You forgot to add the GST to my bill."

Brendan J. O'Byrne

"I knew it was loaded."

"As Leader of the Opposition, I want to say I think the Throne Speech was excellent in every detail."

Doug Broderick

"My opponent is far better qualified than me."

"The neighbours say the convicted serial killer was a
loud man who had parties all the time."

"Oh, we supply that service free at this bank."

"You know, Toronto audiences aren't the best. I
don't love you, Toronto, and good night."

"My merchandise looks terrible on you. Take it off
and just get out."

"It's not the humidity. It's the heat."   *Dale Scaife*

"Vive la Saskatchewan libre!"   *Paulette Moeller*

"Sure I'd like a woman to succeed me as Pope."
                                        Mike England

"I am entering public life so that I can spend less time
with my family."   *Dave Duncan*

"I feel badly about losing the case. Forget about my
bill."   *Robert Campbell*

"You are right, our bank's service charges are
absurd."   *Mark A. Kubisz*

"I'd like a reduction in my wages, please. I'm just too
   highly paid for what I do."

"Austerity should start at the top. As CEO, I should
   take the first and deepest wage cut."   *Alison Motluk*

"Actually, I don't think we have a car on the lot that
   would suit your needs. Sorry."   *Jennifer Duholke*

"Yes, you're right. As a matter of fact, you have too
   much life insurance."   *Brian Yamashita*

"Your tax return was such a learning experience for
   our staff that we are refunding your cheque."
                                              Sydney W. Clay

"Today's special is fresh lake trout, but I don't
   recommend it."   *Jack Orbaum*

"No, sir, we don't require any identification to cash
   this cheque. Your honest face is more than
   sufficient."   *Peter Forbath*

"It's not your fault my son isn't learning anything in
   your class, Miss Brown. He just isn't very bright."

"My company knows this drug has harmful
   side-effects, but it is making too much profit from it
   to take it off the market."

"You're absolutely right, Dad. I am too young to
   learn to drive the car."   *Nancy Goldring*

"Yes, the buns are stale. In fact, if you look more
    closely you'll notice they have freezer burns, too."
"I agree the chef should be embarrassed, but
    customers complain so often he's used to it."
"Yes, we did take you for an idiot when we replaced
    your new battery with a used one."   *Barbara Lougheed*

"My lawyer's bill was very reasonable."
"Never mind my rights, what about my
    responsibilities?"   *Al Wilkinson*

"Of course I've had too much to drink, dear."
"Thank you for stopping me, officer, I shouldn't have
    been speeding."   *Pat Wiffen*

"Hi, we're your next-door neighbours. Could you
    please turn your stereo up?"
"I brought all the tools I need to fix your plumbing."
"Sorry, I have no photos of my grandchildren."
    Alanna Little

"Actually, it ought to be even cheaper. It used to be a
    taxi."   *K.C. Angus*

"As a tourist in your beautiful country, I am
    honoured to help reduce your national deficit via
    my GST contribution."   *Shelly McQuillen*

"Of course I was with another woman. Did you think
    I was at an all-night business meeting?" *Gennie Choban*

"You were here first. I'll park across the street."
    P.D. Peacock

"Don't worry about your dog's barking at midnight.
   It always puts me to sleep."
"I'm sorry, I must have miscounted. I'll get out of the
   express checkout line immediately."   *Charles Crockford*

"You're right, I probably won't respect you in the
   morning."   *Art Stow*

"Of course no one here minds if you smoke."
   Terry L. Charlebois

"I'm terribly sorry our yard is so messy and you have
   to look at the junk heap. We'll clean it up right
   away."
"I'm sorry, I dented your fender. I've waited ages for
   you to come out so I could make it right for you."
   Mary Bonnycastle

"You're right, sir, your chimney doesn't need
   cleaning."   *Les Holroyd*

"Only $400 to repair my bicycle? What a delightful
   surprise."   *Eric Adams*

"As your elected representative, I promise that my
   primary concern will be to remain in office at all
   costs."   *Robert M. Collins*

"Mom, Dad, would you mind turning down that rock
   and roll music? I'm trying to read."   *Michael C. Mayo*

From a dentist: "Now this is going to hurt like hell."
   Morton S. Rapp

Limericks

*It wasn't enough that readers were asked to write
limericks; they had to write clean limericks, suitable for
printing in a daily newspaper. Surprisingly, they made it
look easy. It helps to know that TMR is the abbreviation
for Town of Mount Royal in Montreal, and that
Clayoquot Sound in British Columbia is pronounced
Clack-wit.*

There was a young lady from Wawa,
Northwest of the Canyon Agawa,
Who toured through the East
And never was *triste*,
Except in St-Louis-du-Ha! Ha!   *Gordon Campbell*

The heroes who fought at Long Sault,
Adam Daulac and his crault,
Battled the hordes
With muskets and swords,
Then died, which was sad, so bault hault.   *Isobel Barron*

Suzuki has rare civic pride,
And litter he cannot abide.
His grounds are so neat
The birds wipe their feet
Before they dare enter inside.   *Frank O'Brien*

An angry young man from The Pas
Once poked the PM in the jas.
He said, "Pardon my spleen
But that CF-18
Is something that sticks in my cras."

A lass from the TMR
Once grew an embarrassing b.
For her friend at McGill
With the fine fencing skill
Had no scabbard surrounding his f.   *Michael Freeman*

A certain obscure politician
Who went by the name of Hnatyshyn,
When appointed G.G.,
Pronounced that to be
In accordance with Tory tradition.   *E.H. Thring*

...before they dare enter inside.

There was an old man from Macadam
Who said to his housekeeper, "Madam,
We enjoyed our fish cakes,
But where are our steaks?"
To which she retorted, "You've had 'em."

There was a bold cowboy from Whitehorse
Who never could stay on the right horse.
He'd ride out on a bay
And come back on a grey
And his life was one long female nighthorse.

There was a young man from North York
Who tried eating soup with a fork.
On the seventeenth try
He remarked, with a sigh,
"I wish I had ordered roast pork."   *Edward Baxter*

A judicial lady named Kim
Showed off shoulders both lovely and slim.
And then for a lark,
So did Joe Clark,
But nobody photographed him.   *Geoff Williams*

The cabinet member named Campbell
Is taking an imprudent gamble.
If she fumbles that hook,
We'll all get a look
At her torts and her briefs and preamble.   *B.F. Ryan*

There was a fine diner of York
Who consumed everything with a fork.
When it came to the wine,
He managed just fine
By spearing and sucking the cork.

There was a young priest from Smith's Falls
Who wrote limericks on the church walls.
Quote the bishop, "My son,
You may think this is fun,
But the naughtiness simply appalls."

There was a young lady of Dutton
Whose dresses were made of light cotton;
But when the wind blew,
And high her skirt flew,
It was easy to see what she'd not on.   *David Thomas*

There was a young lady of Spuzzum
Who kept a pet asp in her buzzum.
When warned, "It'll bite!"
She replied, "Well, it might
But forget cans of mace: This outduzzum."

                                        Sarah Stockdale

There was a young fellow from Guelph
Who was madly in love with himself.
He would tell every date
He was ever so great
Which is why he is still on the shelf.   *Steve Paulsson*

A journalist born in Port Credit
Bought a 15-foot python and fed it
A brand new P.C.
Running Word Perfect 3,
But he could not persuade it to edit.

A suit-maker born in Grand Falls
Concentrated his efforts on talls.
He said it's not much
But the shape of the crotch
Has a fantastic impact on comfort.   *Tim and Sheila Andrew*

We're Canada, land of the fir.
Like vichyssoise, that's what we are.
No spice worth a hoot,
And chilly to boot,
And a very tough mixture to stir.   *Gordon Findlay*

Riding Via Rail east, *c'est la vie*.
You arrive *à côté* the Queen E.
There's no clickety-clack
As you "zoom" down the track,
But it sure ain't the French TGV.   *Ed Fennell*

There was a contestant from Clayoquot
Who thought that his entry might layoquot,
But spelling indigenous
Made the whole thing vertiginous.
No judge could dismiss it as hayoquot.   *David Dunsmuir*

There was a young lady from Sydenham
Who loved cupboards and frequently hid in 'em.
But it wasn't till she
Was locked in with a he
That she found out what some people did in 'em.

A young man who hailed from Long Sault
Took his girlfriend along to the zault.
When she cried out, "What's that?
Is it some kind of cat?"
He said, "No, dear, it's only a shrault."   *Philip Smith*

A man from Lake Winnipegosis
Was confused by his doctor's prognosis.
When he asked, "Am I dying?",
He was told, "Stop your crying.
You've only got bad halitosis."   *Peter M. Pangman*

A Missus who lived in Coldwater
Remarked to her feminist daughter:
"I won't be called Mizz,
I am what I is,
If anyone knows it I oughter."   *Judy Bowler*

There was an old vicar from Tweed
Who delivered his sermons at speed,
And to his elation
The rapt congregation
Responded by chanting the creed.   *Alan Sharpley*

First Principles

The challenge was to devise a new scientific law or principle. Thanks to Al Wilkinson for the idea. I've incorporated a few responses to a related challenge, to devise a scientific principle, theory or formula related to a prominent individual. That idea came from David Mayerovitch.

The Glad Uncertainty Principle states that the open end of a garbage bag is always at the other end.

Darrell A. Smith

The average woodworking shop will contain nine million pieces of wood left over from previous projects, not one of which will be the right size for the next project.

James Bechtel

A modern marriage is designed to last the life of the household appliances.
The clarity with which radio stations are received varies inversely with the quality of their programs.

Jim Noble

The closer the deadline, the faster the clock ticks.
Unexpected guests never arrive when the house is
tidy.
The greater the number of supermarket shoppers, the
fewer the cashiers on duty.
The shorter your queue at the grocery checkout
counter, the more coupons the shopper ahead of
you will redeem.
If your cat loves the trial-size sample of a new cat
food, once you've stocked your cupboard with it
he'll never eat another morsel. *Alanna Little*

The menu item considered by you, and rejected, will
always appear at the next table looking better than
your meal.
The proof of the wet paint is in the touching.

Jim Young

Twelve socks into the washer, 11 socks out.
Conceit is inversely proportional to its justification.
Long weekends bring rain. *K.C. Angus*

Left to itself, a dog will always lie on the most expensive rug in the house.

The time between turning off the computer and suddenly remembering one more letter you need to write never exceeds 10 milliseconds.

Even a non-scientist can make a policeman appear out of thin air, by making a U-turn on a deserted road. *Morton S. Rapp*

The more complex the laws, the richer the lawyers.

A person's degree of self-confidence is inversely proportional to the amount of experience.

TV transmission only fails during your favourite program.

The client only arrives on time when the salesman is behind schedule.

Geraldo's Ratio: The dumber the TV show, the bigger the ratings. *Al Wilkinson*

The softer the bread, the harder the butter. *Dulcie Snyder*

When the eye fails to find a lost thumbtack, the foot will. *John W. MacDonald*

The chance of interruption of a romantic encounter equals the number of children in the household times the square of the intensity of the passion being expressed. *David P. Ouchterlony*

Possessions expand to fill the space available for their storage. *Sam Shimizu*

The passage of time accelerates with age. *W.N. Horan*

When the principal drops into your class, the
"foolproof" demonstration always fails.

Lorna VanBergen

When one makes an urgent long-distance phone call
to another time zone, it always turns out to be their
lunch hour. *Bill Drysdale*

Appliances always work fine as soon as the
repairman comes.
When you are late for a meeting, you will hit every
red light.
You always get an offer of a better date as soon as
you make other arrangements.
You always find a use for something a minute after
you have irretrievably thrown it away. *Glenn Patterson*

Whatever any government does for the public good
will work to the private disadvantage of every
citizen. *Laurie Hughes*

A teen-ager's choice in clothing is diametrically
opposite to the choice of the parents. *Gillian Cockcroft*

The stick that burns quickest is the one roasting the
hot dog over the campfire. *Paul Robinson*

When taking new initiatives, remember that the
uninitiated always eat the first missionaries, then
they convert. *Michael Godkewitsch*

A golf ball driven through the branches of a tree will
hit the 10-per-cent wood 90 per cent of the time,
and the 90-per-cent air 10 per cent of the time.

R.D. Johnson

First law of flatwater canoeing: Regardless of your
direction of travel, the wind will always be against
you. *Jim Conley*

When you are feeling uncomfortable and decide to
pass wind because there is no one around, there
always is.

An offer of an executive position comes only from a
firm whose president and founder has at least six
sons directly involved in the business. *Charles Crockford*

John Crow's Law: Prosperity yesterday, prosperity
tomorrow, but hardship today. *Eric Etchen*

Otis's First Law: At any one time in a bank of
elevators, they're all going up or all coming down.

Otis's Second Law: It is always those at the back who
want off first. *Paul D. Corbett*

Poll's Theorem: Polls you like are right 19 times out
of 20; polls you dislike are not representative.

David Savage

Gorbachev's Law: The flow of the toothpaste out of
the tube is irreversible. *David Mayerovitch*

In the sorting of laundry, the sum of two socks
    seldom equals one pair.
The books most urgently needed for homework are
    always those forgotten at school.

Carole and Martin Gerson

The nuisance quotient of a child varies inversely with
    its relationship with its victim.   *Andrew Macpherson*

The line you're in is always the slowest. The line next
    to you is always the fastest. If you change lines, the
    rule holds.
The shortest distance between two points is under
    construction.
The only thing you failed to anticipate will be the
    only thing that happens.
The very last ticket is only ever sold to the person
    immediately in front of you.   *Geoffrey P. Charnley*

The last egg always breaks.   *Simon Warder*

The length of time required to mark a student's essay
    varies inversely with its quality.   *C. Burns*

1. The lawyers win.
2. The insurance companies win.
3. In case of dispute with number 2, see number 1.

Ron Grimes

Missing the Point

The challenge was to devise a movie synopsis that somehow misses the point. Two examples were given. Beauty and the Beast: The career of Gaston, a promising athlete, is destroyed by a ferocious monster. The War of the Worlds: A cautionary tale about the damage bacteria can do.

Bambi: A group of hunters succeeds in bringing venison to the table.
Frank Haigh

Battleship Potemkin: An architectural study showing that ramps are less hazardous to pedestrians and perambulators than flights of stairs.
David Antscherl

Casablanca: Airline boarding procedures are deregulated.

Gone With the Wind: Labour laws and agricultural patterns undergo change in the southern United States.
G.R. Thaler

Bonnie and Clyde: A young couple tries to start a business despite familiar obstacles: unco-operative banks, unreliable transportation and the scarcity of repeat customers.   *Alanna Little*

The Robe: A popular carpenter from Nazareth loses a three-year dispute with local authorities.
Fatal Attraction: A successful attorney and his wife overcome a marital problem that could strain their relationship.   *Michael C. Mayo*

Lawrence of Arabia: An Englishman dies on a motorcycle after too many years on camelback.
King Kong: An ape gets mugged on his first visit to New York.   *Charles Siedlecki*

The Silence of the Lambs: A trail-breaking career in fashion design is cut short by police persecution.
Citizen Kane: The perils of inefficient cataloguing; a compulsive collector dies in frustration when he mislays a precious memento in storage.

                    David Dunsmuir

Songs in Waiting

The challenge was to suggest the first drafts of famous song titles, later (mercifully) changed. Since half the fun lies in guessing what the titles became, I haven't included the real versions.

Somewhere Under the Raincoat.
Blue Suede Gloves.
Chief Warrant Officer Pepper's Lonely Hearts Club
    Band.   *David Mayerovitch*

Please, Mr. Letter Carrier.
Mack the Cutting Utensil.
Sittin' on the Dock of Eaton's.   *Barnet Kussner*

Red River Concavity.
An Ignited Universe is Not My Goal.   *Eric Adams*

O Rupertland.   *Don Collier*

Round About the Time the Clock Strikes Twelve.
                                         Alix Vance

I've Got You Under My Fingernails.
What Kind of Foolish Person Do You Think I Am?
This Land is My Personal Patch of Ground.

Wayne Cunningham

Both Sides Instantly.
San Jose Isn't Listed on My Bus Schedule.   *Jenefer Curtis*

I Could Have Danced for Twenty Minutes or So.
Lucy on the Roof With Rhinestones.
Yankee Doodle OK.   *John Greene*

You Light Up My Garage.   *Mary-Ellen Ross*

Smoke Gets in Your Throat.
Yes! We Have No Broccoli.   *Geoff Geduld*

I'll Build a Stairway to the Second Floor.

Margaret McCrank

River of Indeterminate Age and Sex.   *Jim Parr*

Small Change Can't Buy Me Affection.
My Faintly Quirky Valentine.
I Love the Can-Can Capital of France.   *Shelley Gaffe*

By the Time I Get the Kleenex.   *Charles Crockford*

Get Your Kicks on Route 25.
I Did It Just the Way You Said, Okay?   *R.M. Martin*

How Much Tax on that Doggie in the Window?
        Audrey M. Bates

Scarborough Fair/Parsley, Sage, Rosemary and
        Garlic   *Joel Hugen and Nadine Fletcher*

I'm Beholden to You for the Reminiscence.
A Herbal Infusion for a Couple.
We're Economically Advantaged.   *Alanna Matthew*

What is the Precise Nature of Reality, Alfie?
Escalator to Heaven.   *Chris Hurst*

Don't Cry for Me, Uruguay.   *Laurie Hughes*

Don't Fret, Be Glad.
When the Quite Nice People Go Marching In.
I Just Called to Say Let's Do Lunch.
Johnny Behave.   *Barbara Wanless*

I Fall to Disjointed Bits.
Some Vaguely Interesting Evening.   *Martha Keaner*

Somewhere My Significant Other.   *B. Dahlby*

Awesome Grace.
Putting on the Triscuit.
The Maple Leaf for a While, Anyway.   *R.J. Bergman*

Yo, Canada!
I'll Be Down to Get You in a Lada, Honey.   *Jane Brant*

Mr. Tambourine Person.   *Lester Bryon*

It's Irrelevant (If It Doesn't Have That Swing).
    Don Mathieson

Send in the Zambonis.
Don't Let the Sunscreen Run Out on Me.   *Luther Holton*

You Can't Always Get What You Think You're
    Entitled To.   *Alanna Little*

Rhapsody in Chartreuse.
The Age of Virgo.   *Tina M. Brown*

February Song.   *A.E. Eddenden*

You Are My Moonshine.
Greenleggings.   *Don Suthers*

What a Difference a Day Pass Makes.
I'm in the Mood for Liverwurst.
Someone to Watch Over My RSPs.   *Douglas H. Parker*

Lady Comport Yourself Becomingly.
How Shall We Deal With the Inebriated Seafarer?
    K.C. Angus

Skewed Siblings

The challenge was to propose skewed siblings for well-known people. The idea came from David Dunsmuir, who offered, by way of example, Jake Epp's war-hero brother Dee and Ross Perot's tempestuous brother Pross.

Sir Robert Peel's comedian brother, B. Nana.
William Holden's obsequious sister, Bea.
Anton Chekhov's secretary-sister, Mayla.   *Allan Gould*

W.C. Fields' lazy brother, Chester.   *Barbara Mader*

John Major's bearish brother, Ursa.
Teri Garr's flighty sister, Budgeri.   *Daphne Hawkins*

Ralph Klein's rejected brother, Dee.   *Karl Dilcher*

Winona Ryder's equine brother, Orson.   *Jennifer Duholke*

Julie Christie's devout brother, Corpus.   *Procter LeMare*

Joe Ghiz's Scottish brother, Hag.
Roch LaSalle's big brother, Col.
Marcel Masse's affectionate sister, Amoa.
Billy Ocean's thoughtful brother, Ivan.
Mackenzie King's imitative sister, Mimi.
Bobby Fischer's aquatic brother, King.
Mel Brooks' brawling brother, Donny.
Don Getty's Roman sister Spa and his plain sister
    Seren.
Ann Landers' amorous brother, Phil.   *Mike England*

Albert Einstein's monstrous younger brother, Frank.
                                    Michele Ernsting

Pitcher Jim Abbott's vegetarian brother Peter.
Meryl Streep's Hollywood sister Sunset.   *Dave Hook*

Clyde Wells' have-not brother, M.T.   *Stephen Dopp*

Sean Penn's messy brother, Pigg.   *Terry McLeod*

President François Mitterrand's travelling cousin,
    Taxi.   *Don Suthers*

Moses' poorest brother, Oz.   *Peter J. Robinson*

Sheila Copps' troubled brother, Hic.   *Christine Hinchley*

Bob Rae's distant brother, Hoo.   *Frank Gough*

Veronica Tennant's officer brother, Lou.
Brendan Behan's travel-agent sister, Carrie.
Immanuel Kant's poor sister, Mendy.
Robert Redford's car-salesman brother, Rusty.
Faye Dunaway's hermit brother, Hid.
Madonna's operatic sister, Prix.
Woody Allen's cowboy brother, Teng.
Johnny Cash's eruptive brother, Volcani.
Bernadette Peters' dietitian sister, Sue.   *Al Wilkinson*

Salvador Dali's procrastinating sister, Dilly.
Boris Yeltsin's doorkeeper brother, Nobod.
Jane Austen's debilitating brother, Ex.
Mark Twain's steamy sister, Choo-Choo.   *K.C. Angus*

Kirstie Alley's slightly better brother, Margin.

Peter Marucci

Alexander Graham Bell's lightheaded sister, Tinker.
P.D. James' faithful chauffeur brother, Home.
Daniel Boone's simian sister, Bab.   *E. Warren Steiner*

Helmut Kohl's diplomatic sister, Proto.

Phil Gurski and Pat Walsh

Couplets

The challenge was to compose rhyming couplets with lines not exceeding three words. This tricky assignment was set courtesy of K.C. Angus.

Make food last;
Don't eat, fast.

L.E. Jones

Deshabille is greater
Nearer the Equator.

Cherry Watson

Corporations love NAFTA.
Workers don't hafta.

Eusebio L. Koh

Mozart or Haydn?
It's difficult decaydn.

Extinct's Tyrannosaurus Rex.
Reason? Insufficient sex.

Jim Parr

Sheep in barns
Usually tell yarns.

John Belbeck

Every chicken begs:
Don't eat eggs.

John Belbeck

Applauding her taste,
He lied bare-faced.

Her claiming virginity
Bordered on divinity.

One person's dissolution
Is another's evolution.

R. W. Crosby

Chore of Noah's:
Store the boas.

Object of owl:
Murder most foul.

R. G. MacNeill

Rattle the sabre,
Frighten the neighbour.

Mary Seeman

Not going metric:
Am I eccentric?

Fred Farr

every chicken begs/don't eat eggs

A broker's suggestion
Can cause indigestion.

Don't expect banks
To break ranks.

The Challenge drains
Most people's brains.   *E. Warren Steiner*

A little kiss
Makes life bliss.   *Patrisha Grainger Robertson*

A little tot
Hits the spot.

Mary's little lamb
Turned into Spam.   *Ian D. Brown*

Too many cooks
Keep writing books.   *Mary Dando*

Mousetraps are irrelevant
To the elephant.

Gin and tonic
Makes me laconic.   *Ken Purvis*

National Gallery cognoscenti
Shamelessly pay plenty.   *J.M. Snyder*

Break a diet,
Guilt cells riot.   *Ruth Brown*

Arteries clog pronto
In downtown Toronto.

Glib campaign pledges
Soon become hedges.

Early in Genesis
Appears Adam's nemesis.

TV viewers vote
With their remote.

Guinevere's plights
Caused sleepless knights.

Alanna Little

Adam and Eve
Deserved a reprieve.

Narcoleptics can sleep
Without counting sheep.

Does arson require
A burning desire?

Arthur Lerman

Hate-filled invective
Is rarely objective.

Considering the alternative,
Aging is affirmative.

For seniors, flattery
Recharges one's battery.

Arthur M. Lipman

Three days rain
Brings arthritic pain.

Liquor to fortify
Will often mortify.

Attempts to gladden
Quite often madden.

Marg Gillies

TV's best bet?
Unplug your set.

Car washed again?
Forecast is rain.

"Elvis lives."
What gives?

As checkouts go,
Why's yours slow?

Charles Crockford

Wearing short shorts
Invites rude retorts.

My "significant other"
Doesn't thrill Mother.

Ethel Kesler

With cellular phone
You're never alone.

Alanna Matthew

What's in a Place Name

In their book The Deeper Meaning of Liff, Douglas Adams and John Lloyd devised ingenious definitions for ordinary place names. The challenge was to do likewise, using Canadian place names.

Bawlf (v): To weep loudly and melodramatically for the sake of being noticed.

Vonda (n, masc & fem): One given to frequent bawlfing.

Elko (adj, informal): Crazed or deranged following a long stay in the wilderness.

Gleichen (n): Any minor dings to a luxury automobile's paintwork that occur during the first fortnight of ownership.

Hixon (n): A person bound or appointed to deliver bad news.

Ogoki (n): The unshakable sensation that the trousers you're wearing are too short.

Gerry L'Orange

Wawa (n): The self-congratulatory movement men make when they rearrange their trousers in the front.

Abitibi (n): The bits of food that drop out of your sandwich when you bite it.

Blanc-Sablon (n): The mountain of used tissues that pile up in a wastepaper basket when you have a raging cold.

Nipigon (n): A thread escaping from the eye of a needle.

Antigonish (n): The irritating itch you get under your bike helmet, or in the middle of your back when you're wearing a thick parka and have your arms full of groceries.

Bawlf (v): The infuriating way plastic forks refuse to pierce anything of substance.

Burlington (n): Five o'clock shadow as reflected in the stainless steel of an everyday object, e.g. a toaster.

Esterhazy (n): The blowing of wisps of snow in waves on the road behind the car directly ahead of you.

Okanagan (adj.): A doorknob that's hanging on at an angle.   *Isabel Bliss*

grimsby (n.): that sinking feeling you get when you can't think of an answer on an exam.

Banff (n): Forced exhalation, as when hit in the
abdomen.

Squamish (n): A feeling of nausea. *Geoffrey Hopkinson*

Neepawa (n): A large, flightless bird native to
Carleton County. *John Gilbert*

Yarker (v): To make a short, amusing story very long
and very boring. *Peter Garnett*

[Cape] Freels (n): The little, sharp bits of hair always
left under the collar after a haircut.

Welchpool (n): The puddle under the floormat on the
driver's side in winter.

Keefers (n): The self-perpetuating and non-removable
kinks in a telephone cord.

Musquash (n): The substance found in the bottom of
the vegetable crisper drawer in the fridge.

Nimpkish (n): The over-the-shoulder glance of a
just-chastised child who thinks you are not looking.

Govenlock (n): The pathetic swatch of hair combed
from well down the side in order to cover a bald
pate.

Arcola (n): The little hole between the inner tines of a
fish fork. *Wayne Harvey*

Napanee (n): A disposable-diaper landfill site.

Ogoki (n): An insect bite, in a tender spot, acquired
while skinny-dipping.

Omemee (n): One who whines tirelessly and without
success about his or her supposed grievance.

Wasaga (n): Plastic detritus washed up on a beach.

Michael Johnson

Halifax (n): A long-distance breathalyzer.   *H. Metszies*

Timiskaming (n): The feeling of discomfort you get
  in the first half hour of wearing new shoes.
Chibougamou (n): Reference to the ongoing debate
  as to whether a cow lies down front legs first or
  hind legs first.
Kenso (n): The ancient art of folding napkins.
Perth (n): Starting a sentence and failing to finish it.

Sally Thornton

Squamish (v): To desperately attempt to save face
  after a strongly stated opinion has been debunked.
Manitowaning (n): The sound of a canoeist's paddle
  moving through perfectly still water on a moonlit
  lake.   *David Marmorek*

Tatamagouche (n): Residual sock fluff caught
  between toes.
Annapolis Royal (n): A dessert made with
  rum-soaked apples and vanilla ice cream.
Kanata (n): The inability to balance a chequebook.
Huronia (n): The accumulation of excessive material
  wealth.   *Karen Janigan*

Oshawa (n): The sound of a leaky galosh being taken
  off.   *Gerald La Fontaine*

Coquitlam (n): Unstable period of rule in which ministers of ruling party resign en masse.

Kamloops (n): Letter delivered to the wrong address more than once.

Namu (n): Situation in which an appointed meeting place could be any of two or more possibilities.

Haney (n): Determined stare pedestrians must use at crosswalks to persuade cars to stop.   *C.M. Squire*

Yarmouth (n): Long-winded old codger full of local lore.   *Gertrude Gunn*

Winkler (n): A lawn sprinkler that works intermittently.   *Charles Crockford*

Kitchener (n): A food-wolfing kid who perpetually hangs out by the refrigerator.

Drumheller (n): A rock band's percussionist gone totally out of control.   *Eileen Morris*

Chilliwack (n): A cold snap.   *Michael Hadley*

Buctouche (n): An explosive nasal sound, usually made while fumbling for a Kleenex.

Guelph (n): The sound made by a person walking through marshland while wearing loose overshoes.
          Jack Cobb

Edrans (n): The feeling engendered when a sneeze vanishes just as one has readied oneself for it.
          Matt Stevenson

Hybrid
Quotations

The challenge was to devise hybrid quotations from two well-known people or characters.

A rose is a rose is a rose by any other name would smell as sweet. — Gertrude Shakespeare.

Arthur Lerman

Big Brother is watching you do something to me. — Cole Orwell.
I have a dream, dream-dream-dreee-em. — Martin Luther Everly.
I'm so lonely I could cry "God for Henry! England and St. George!" — Hank Shakespeare.
Tune in, turn on, drop out, out brief candle. — Timothy Shakespeare.

Allan Gould

England expects every man to do his Judy, Judy, Judy. — Horatio Grant.

H.S. Ferguson

The buck stops here, where the deer and the antelope
   play. — Truman/Higley.
Beauty's but skin deep and crisp and even. —
   Davies/Neale.   *R.G. MacNeill*

A journey of a thousand miles starts with one giant
   step for mankind. — Confucius/Armstrong.
Out, damned Spot; run, Spot, run. — The Lady
   Macbeth Reader.   *Chris Sri*

Man is born free, but everywhere he is in chain
   stores. — Jean Jacques Ghermezian.
It is a riddle wrapped in a mystery inside an enigma;
   and the answer is ... ? — Alex Trebek Churchill.
                                          Linda Lumsden

Would you believe an iron curtain? — Don Adams/
   Churchill.   *Jim Chick*

I think, therefore I am not a crook. — René Nixon.
Water, water everywhere that Mary went. — Samuel
   Taylor Goose.
Once more into the breach, dear friends, and
   influence people. — Henry Carnegie V.   *K.C. Angus*

His life was gentle, and the elements so mixed in him
that Nature might stand up and say to all the
world, "Go ahead. Make my day." — Dirty
Antony.

Please, sir, I want some more; do I dare to eat a
peach? — J. Alfred Twist.

The envelope, please. What find I here? Fair Portia's
counterfeit. — Bassanio on Oscar night. *Fred Farr*

Love means never having to say you're dethpicable.
— Daffy Segal.

The foxes have holes and the birds of the air have
nests, but I am not an animal, I am a human being.
— Jesus Merrick. *Helen McCusker*

To be or not to be, what is the question? — Hamlet
Trebek.

How do I love thee? I *love* to *count* the vays. —
Elizabeth Barrett Browning/The Count of Sesame
Street. *Michael Catling*

I have not yet begun the Beguine. — John Paul
Porter. *Chris Hurst*

Go ahead: Make my 15 minutes. — Dirty Harry
Warhol.

Kiss me, Ollie. — Admiral Stanley Horatio Laurel.
David Dunsmuir

Dr. Livingstone, I presume. What's up, Doc? —
Stanley B. Bunny. *David Philip*

Whither thou goest, I will go, but I'll still have the
feelin' that I wanted to stay! — Ruth Durante.
Come on up and just watch me some time. — Mae
Trudeau.
I bring you peace in our time but *still* I don't get no
respect! — Rt. Hon. Sir Neville Dangerfield.
Th-th-th-that's all folks, but I shall return. — Porky
MacArthur.   *Glen Acorn*

Four score and seven beers ago ... — W.C. Lincoln.
                                           Peter Marucci

It isn't over until the fat lady sings, "O that this too
too solid flesh would melt." — Yogi Berra Hamlet.
To sleep, perchance to dream the impossible dream.
— Hamlet Quixote.   *Ken Purvis*

It it were done when 'tis done t'were well it were
done when time is on my side. — Mick
Shakespeare.   *T. Cranford*

Aaa...CHOO! Brute. — Sneezy Caesar.
Beauty is tooth, tooth booty. — Tooth Fairy Keats.
Yabba dabba doo as you would be done by. — Fred
Chesterfield.   *Cherry Watson*

Come into the garden, Maud, for I am not as other
men. — Tennyson/Pharisee.
Jenny kissed me when we met, not with a bang but a
whimper. — Hunt/Eliot.   *Jim Parr*

Ask not what my country can do for me. Ask what I
can do for my country on $5 a day. — John F.
Frommer   *Ian D. Brown*

Barbed
Apologies

The challenge, suggested by Graham Jones, was to compose a forced apology containing the hint of a further insult. A number of readers submitted one old favourite: "I was wrong when I said you weren't fit to eat with pigs."

"I'm sorry. Had I known you were going to lose, I wouldn't have won by a mile." *Elizabeth Macey*

"I'm sorry. I was wrong when I said your photos weren't worth blowing up." *Sandra Crosson*

"I'm sorry, it was cruel of me to say that you are totally brainless." *Ruth Brown*

"I didn't mean to interrupt. I hadn't realized you
were saying anything."

"Sorry, minister. I ought to have known that such a
controversial comment was the work of your
speechwriter."   *Jim Parr*

"I regret calling you a halfwit, but in the heat of
argument I tend to exaggerate."   *K.C. Angus*

"I apologize, you're not as stupid as you look."
                                                        J.R. Martin

"I'm sorry I called you an ignoramus. That means a
dummy."   *Ed Kamps*

"I'm sorry for spilling the ink on your tie, though for
a moment I thought the spot improved the look of
it."

"I apologize for inadvertently trespassing on your
lawn. I had no cause to do so, since our boundary
is so well marked; my lawn is so much greener and
has no dandelions."   *Glen Acorn*

"I'm sorry I didn't seem to be listening to you. I was
thinking about something interesting."
"I'm sorry that bullet just missed you. I'm really a
terrible shot."   *Michael Davies*

"So sorry you thought I had been inadvertently rude."
"I'm sorry I said your opinion was based on very
little knowledge. That, of course, was an
exaggeration."
"Oops, sorry it broke. Don't they make things
shoddily nowadays."
"Sorry, I forgot we had met before. I have a terrible
memory for trivia."
"Sorry I ate the last cookie, but you're probably better
off without it."   *Alanna Little*

"I'm sorry I offended your family. When I said your
late sister was the stupidest person in this town, I
regret I did not give due consideration to her
surviving relatives."   *Jeffrey White*

"Sorry for the delay. I'll waste no time in reading
your résumé."   *Simon Warder*

"My apologies. I was wrong when I said you were as
much use as a hole in the ground."   *David Savage*

"I'm sorry I got doggy-do on your white carpet, but
your doormat was worn out."   *Joyce Edwards*

Minus a Letter

The challenge was to remove one letter from a sentence to comic effect. The idea came from Ken Purvis, whose examples included: Because they had paid for their misdeeds, they were known as the Pirates of Penance.

Columbus, ever the frugal explorer, crossed the
    Atlantic using just three gallons.   *Alix Vance*

Foot fetishist exposed in sex sandal.
His face spread into a welcoming gin.
Cereal producers hold branstorming session.   *Jim Parr*

The new homeowner knew intuitively that he had a
    case against the unscrupulous contractor, but he
    just couldn't find the roof.
Unaccountably, he feels much safer having sex in a
    condo.   *R. W. Crosby*

Fatty fast foods are a gut on the market.   *P. McLeod*

The church choir is going to sin to raise money for
    the new organ.   *Diane Bethune*

Children love to hear Bible stories, like how God
 crated the world in six days and then took a rest.
His doctor warned him that if he didn't take better
 care of his heath he'd soon be six feet under ground.
It's wise to wear an insulated vet when hunting in the
 fall.
Of all Canada's symbols, surely that of the male tree
 is the most exciting.
The nervous dinner guest was so concerned about
 where to sit that she pulled out her neighbour's hair
 by mistake.
I'm so inexperienced about games, I can't tell one cad
 from another. *Kathy Hooke*

The cheese salesman kept samples in his brie case.
God spoke to Moses from a burning bus. *David Barker*

Dracula? Think of him as your usual blood-sucking
 lech. *Mossie Hancock*

He says this diet is the hardest thin he has ever done.
 Peter Brodie

the cheese salesman kept
samples in his brie case.

Summer romances are usually just affairs of the heat.

Phil Gurski

The queen sat upon her throne as the magnificent royal crow was carefully placed upon her head.

Basia Bales

The Three Musketeers were renowned for their sophisticated wordplay.
Prior to the current period, Canada was a British colon.
In court, the poultry farmer was defended by a prominent layer.
The drug dealer shipped marijuana by Canada Pot.

Al Wilkinson

The federal Tories have run out of team.

David Dunsmuir

Please make sure that the after-dinner speaker is properly tanked.
Pavlov trained his dogs in such a way that ringing a bell brought about salvation.
I caught this young rascal peeing through the keyhole.
The gondoliers were charged with having canal knowledge.
The entire track team disappeared without a race.

Edward Baxter

Las Vegas is like the U.S. flag because it has stars and strips.
The car-rental agent's mother always told him to say "lease" and "thank you."   *Marilyn Penner*

My overly indulgent cousin insists on bringing her
   rats over to play with my children.
It was fat that attracted John to her.   *Ruth Brown*

Among the most disappointing entries at a recent film
   festival were 10 Canadian premiers.   *Helga Wachsmuth*

The waiter piled spaghetti on the bald man's pate.
He had worked previously in Ottawa at the
   Department of Eternal Affairs.   *Martin Galvin*

The milliner and her assistant had a long love-hat
   relationship.
The banker accused his client of being insolent.
Arriving on Parliament Hill, the new Prime Minister
   went directly to the power room.
The fun-loving guard enjoyed working with the
   criminally inane.   *Robert Hudgins*

The batter stepped up to the plate and waited for the
   itcher to stop scratching.   *Terry McFarland*

One of the cannibal's fondest childhood memories
   was the smell of a freshly baked oaf.   *D. Kenny*

What a party! They danced till dawn on the pizza.
                   Procter LeMare

The first thing the student did was choose his curses
   for the year.   *Charles Crockford*

In the heat of fiery battle, King Richard cried, "My
   kingdom for a hose!"   *Gloria Ellenton*

Rather than cry over spilt milk, try to recup your
    losses.   *Sandra Frayne*

A first-rate reader can bring an old Tory to life.
                        Dorothy J. Rule

After three successive tee shots landed in the lake,
    Anne threw away her iron and grabbed her diver.
                      Bryan Scully

Attempting to create a non-artisan atmosphere,
    convention organizers have decided to exclude
    sculptors and cabinet-makers.   *Alexandre Menard*

The Japanese emperor enjoyed hunting ducks with
    his shogun.
When the prodigal son returned home, his father
    killed the fated calf.
She dieted and exercised regularly, in the hope of
    acquiring a beautiful boy.
Because of her fondness for red wine, she often spent
    her holidays in pain.   *R.M. Baxter*

When Oedipus Rex learned what had happened, you
    could have knocked him down with a father.
                      A. Taylor

Ebenezer Scrooge feared the host of Christmas past.
                      J.D. Cambridge

What we will remember most about our trip to
    Mexico were the incredible runs.   *Marina Kelton*

The meticulous carpenter worked at a nail's pace.

Garry and Lyra Pappin

Regular spaying will rid your kitchen of unwelcome
    pets.
Noah was determined to save as many animals as
    possible from the terrible food.
The English language is rich because it employs so
    many nuns.   *Ken Purvis*

The minister vowed to address homelessness with
    more public hosing.
The explorers were welcomed by the naive population.
Increased consumer spending should simulate
    economic recovery.   *Alanna Little*

She tried to enjoy the film, but his vice was much too
    distracting.   *R. W. Carnahan*

Political life is cut and trust.
The strategies of the caucus were beyond the ken of
    moral men.
The NHL player, speared by a stick and slammed on
    the boards, was living a harmed life.   *Charles Bastomsky*

At a vermiculture auction, the early bid gets theworm.

Peter Marucci

Grasping both tables as best he could, Moses
    struggled down the mountain.
The old chef seldom slept on those nights his dog was
    baking.   *Shawn McSweeny*

The castratos were cut kids.   *K.C. Angus*

Spoonerisms

The challenge was to turn the title of a book, play or movie into a spoonerism — transposing the first letter(s) of words or syllables — and briefly explain the plot. Thanks to Audrey M. Bates for the idea.

For Whom the Tell Bowls: William gives up archery
    for lawn-bowling.   *Diane Bethune*

The Born Thirds: Psychology of the third child.
                               Ann Aylward

The Bled and the Rack: Sixteen ways to cook lamb.
The Mart of the Hatter: An exciting new scheme to
    revitalize the economy of lower Spadina Avenue in
    Toronto.   *Don Stevenson*

Hat on a Cotton Roof: The saga of a haberdasher
    who works out of a tent.   *Peter Marucci*

Little Tan Mate: Sequel to Crocodile Dundee,
    featuring Dundee's diminutive, sun-worshipping
    sidekick.   *Kelvin Leddy*

She Conks to Stupor: Self-defence techniques for the urban woman.   *Alanna Matthew*

Rushing it in the Buff: Sex in a cold climate.
                    Shirley Mann Gibson

The Gaudy Bard: Shakespeare in Technicolor.
                    Walter Blackburn

Ringing in the Seine: French technologists develop underwater cellular phone.   *Frank Haigh*

A Vroom With a Ewe: How to transport sheep by racing car.   *Colin Norman*

A Sale of Two Titties: The biography of Madonna.
                    Lois Halls

Pin Tweaks: An unhappy incident in the life of an inept seamstress.   *The Crawford, Galea and Merry families*

born with a silver spoonerism
in his mouth.

Radars of the Lost Irk: Ever forget what annoyed
you? This video will help you access those elusive
feelings.

Buy Bligh Booze: An abortive attempt to take over
the Bounty by getting the captain drunk.

Didier Bergeret

All the Mings' Ken: An encyclopedia of ancient
Chinese knowledge. *Arthur Lerman*

The Knee of the Idle: A study of immobility.

Ken Norwich

The Scarlet Teller: A blushing banker learns to deal
with society's scorn. *John & Wren Brouwer*

Fenry the Hourth: Story of a talking equine with a
small speech impediment. *Michael Davies*

Collective Nouns

The challenge was to enrich the language with new collective nouns. The idea for the contest came from Penny Anagnostopoulos, and Ivan Hrabowsky sent in photostats from a few pages of James Lipton's book An Exaltation of Larks — the ultimate in collective nounery. Maurice Whitby attached an Associated Press report of a similar contest in the U.S. magazine Wildlife, which yielded a dash of cheetahs, a battery of electric eels and a pinch of crabs.

A harangue of constitutional experts.   *J.M. Hibberd*

An ostentation of Torontonians.   *Margaret Greaves*

A fabrication of gnus.   *E. Warren Steiner*

A tontine of bicycle couriers.   *Martha Keaner*

A division of mathematicians.   *Phil Gurski and Pat Walsh*

A clique of tap dancers.
A brood of hamlets.   *Glenn Kubish*

A ruffle of ballerinas.
A compulsion of gamblers.   *John W. Cruickshank*

A chain of lynx.
A can of optimists.   *Gwyn Richards*

A shiver of nudists.   *Don Suthers*

An inevitability of aphids.   *Pat Ajello*

A slew of executioners.
A foundation of bricklayers.   *Diane Mackie*

A sullen of teen-agers.   *Murray Logan*

A suggestion of hypnotists.   *Michael Root*

A congregation of Sunday shoppers.
A skulk of cross-border shoppers.   *Kurt Loeb*

A sixpack of hunters.   *Hugh Whitney*

a diet of worms

A conceit of car phones.   *Marjorie C. Bacon*

A bozo of clowns.
A quackle of ducks.   *Howard Jones*

An idiocy of talk-show hosts.   *Maureen Griffiths*

A posterior of cyclists.   *M. Bone*

A showing of realtors.   *Brian Hale*

A sweat of bush pilots.   *Bruce Gordon*

A stampede of philatelists.   *Margaret Caines*

An embarrassment of witches.   *Frank Haigh*

A snarl of paper clips.   *Josie Chapman-Smith*

A gross of special effects.
A month of Hyundais.   *Dave Ashby*

An insult of TV commercials.   *Morris Love*

An aggression of taxicabs.   *Robert J. Patton*

A Tigger of hyperactive children.
A gloom of tax accountants.   *Donald M. White*

I, You, They

The challenge was to devise a "first-person, second-person, third-person" equation along these lines: My home has a casual decor; yours has that lived-in look; hers is a mess. Alanna Little supplied the idea and example.

I enhance my highlights; you experiment with colour; she has black roots.

My children are energetic; yours are a challenge; hers are out of control.

I drive responsibly; you avoid accidents; he brakes for green lights.

I absorb documentaries; you enjoy sitcoms; he's a couch potato.
Julie Blanchette

My artwork is a unique balance of originality and echoes from the past; your work is interesting, but highly derivative; his work is uninspired and outright plagiarism.
Russell Yapp

I am pious; you are fanatical; they are superstitious.
David Mayerovitch

I have an inquiring mind; you have a natural
  curiosity; she's nosy.   *Don Scanlan*

I am unpopular; you are disliked; he is the Prime
  Minister.   *S.F. Sommerfeld*

My singing is okay for church; yours is a little off-key;
  he's flat.
I'm careful with a dollar; you pinch pennies; she's a
  miser.
I'm into cocooning; you like a quiet life; she's dull.
I'm fashion-conscious; you accessorize; she's
  over-dressed.   *Andrea S. Cunningham*

I feel okay this morning; you were quite funny last
  night; he has really turned into a lush.
                                      William Lawrence

I'm making an offer; you're making demands; he's
  holding us for ransom.   *Steve Paulsson*

pious   fanatical   superstitious

I prefer a known path; you are set in your ways; he is
  pigheaded.
I am precise; you are deliberate; she never gets
  anything done.
I am enthusiastic; you are zealous; she is a fanatic.

Bob and Christine Goodnough

My spelling is creative; my colleague's spelling is
  erratic; our students' spelling is terrible.   *Mary Vipond*

I support worthy causes; you buy lottery tickets; he
  gambles.   *Margaret Zubert*

My garden is an example of mixed Victorian
  horizontal banking; your garden has an interesting
  cross-section of plantings; her garden is packed
  with blooming weeds.
My two-year-old grandson learns life skills through
  self-expression; your grandson is rather negative;
  her grandson can't say anything but "no!"   *Kay Dills*

I look distinguished; you don't show your years; he
  looks old and grey.
My brother is an individualist; your brother is
  eccentric; his brother is weird.
My daughter is extremely popular; your daughter
  plays the field; his daughter is a tramp.

Charles Crockford

I like women; you are libidinous; he is a sex maniac.

Tom Ainslie

I am a romantic; you are a flirt; he is a lecher.
I have an open mind; you can never make decisions;
  he hasn't a clue.   *Arthur M. Lipman*

I made an understandable error; you kinda goofed; he
  is a dunderhead.   *Morton S. Rapp*

I'm feeling a pleasant glow; you're getting drunk; he's
  bombed out of his mind.   *Russell Yapp*

I have a trendy haircut; you experiment with your
  hair; his hair is grotesque.   *Martha Keaner*

I'm elegantly slim; you're a trifle skinny; she's
  anorexic, poor thing.
I'm interested in human affairs; you're a bit of a
  gossip; she's a real tattle-tale.
In my case it's mostly muscle; well, you're nicely
  upholstered; she should go for liposuction.
                                                 Procter LeMare

Titles, All Dressed

The challenge was to adapt the title of a book, poem, play or film to give it a bit more clothes sense. The examples offered included Mutiny on the Bow Tie and How Green Was My Valet. Many readers suggested Jurassic Parka.

In Search of XL Lengths   *W.C. Cherwinski*

Just Sew Stories
Battle Hem of the Republic
They Shoot Housecoats, Don't They?   *Mary Jean Ricci*

The Magnificent Size Seven
Tunics of Glory
The Apparels of Pauline   *Sue Dulley*

Gulliver's Trousers
The Pelican Briefs   *D. Charles Roy*

Bonnets for the Portuguese   *Betsy Newbeck*

Tights Andronicus
Boys 'N' the Snood
Monocle Antoine
The Velours and the Horror   *Phyllis and Al Erlenbusch*

Snow White and the Seven Drawers
La Bohèmeline   *Brendan O'Byrne*

Slipless in Seattle   *Susan James*

Polyestergeist
Rayon Man   *Robert Davis*

Scarf Face
A Tailor of Two Cities   *Kevin McAvoy*

Panties Inferno   *Philip Thornhill*

Twenty Thousand Leotards Under the Sea
A Zipper Runs Through It   *Helen McCusker*

A Timely History of Briefs
Francis Coppola's Accessorize Now!   *John Lamont Jr.*

a zipper runs through it.

Levis of Girls and Women	*Margaret Toth*
Alice in Wonder-Bra	*Philip Pinkus*
A Streetcar Named Dior	*F. Gunn*
Ties My Father Sold Me	*Merrick family*
Diet for a Small Pant Suit	*Sandra Frayne*
Bodystocking of Evidence Terry Cloth and the Pirates	*Wayne Cunningham*
The Cruel See-Through	*Alanna Little*
Who's Afraid of Virgin Wool?	*Maria Grossi*
The Greatest Shawl Unearthed	*Dena Stockburger*
Glove is a Many-Fingered Thing	*Bob Termuende*
The Holy Bib	*Vern and Eleanor Gilbert*
Vile Bodice	*Kurt Loeb*
For Whom the Belt Holds	*John Sullivan*
When Florsheim Met Bally Mary Bobbins	*Sara Berger*
Silence of the Looms	*Ilan Kelman*
Pelisse Academy Caftans Courageous	*Jo Ann Blondal and John Bishopric*

The Wash That Rends the Nightie
The World According to GAP   *Ken Purvis*

The Clothing of the American Mind   *Con Sieben*

Don't Shoe the Piano Player
I Remember Muumuu   *Irma Coucill*

Kingsley Amis's Lucky Gymslip   *Ray Stringer*

Das Gumboot   *Morgan Roebuck*

Danskin With Wolves   *Heather Peacock*

Kidnappies   *F.M. Murphy*

Hook! (and Eye)
Les Lingeries Dangereuses   *Richard Holland*

The King and Eyewear
Moby Dickey   *John Ricker*

The Hitchhiker's Guide to Gucci   *Will Easton*

Ivanhose   *Gina Calleja*

Two Gentlemen of Velcro   *Trevor J. Harvey*

The Houndstooth of the Baskervilles
Suspenders in the Grass
To Kill a Mackintosh   *Earl Liu*

Puttin' on the Mitts   *Jeff McLeod*

Haltered States
Wool Street   *Jim Ballinger*

The Closet of the American Mind   *Laurie Konwinski*

The Three Faces of Yves
Blackwell's Beauty   *Janet Mendelsohn*

The Britches of Eastwick   *Barbara Humphries*

Sleeveless in Seattle   *Sarah Compton*

The Hunt for Red Organza   *Glenora Tite*

Separate Labels
Barefoot in the Parka   *Louise Rich*

T.S. Eliot's The Waistband   *R. Moran*

The Wizard of Gauze
2001: A Lace Odyssey   *Paul and Maureen Dunseath*

Socks and the Single Girl
Turtleneck Diary   *Glenn Patterson*

The Kama Suitrack   *Deanna Silverman*

Doublet Indemnity   *S.F. Sommerfeld*

The Robe Less Ravelled   *Eric Mendelsohn*

Tolkien's Lord of the Earrings
Knickerless Nickerby   *Martyn Ward*

Ruthless Rhymes

Writer Harry Graham was known for ruthless rhymes that imagined unusual reactions to death, accidents and the like. I invited readers to write a four-line poem in that spirit, and composed this example: "When Jacky, playing too near the side, / Fell off the roller-coaster ride, / The management, in sympathy, / Let Jacky's mother ride for free." Readers without a taste for black humour should consider themselves warned. To my mind, a few of these are as good as Graham's best.

When Tom fell on the kitchen fire,
Which soon became his funeral pyre,
Mama said, "Dinner will be late.
The guests must come at nine, not eight."

The thunder cracked. The lightning struck
Poor Freddie's Blue Grass Towing truck.
And folks came in from far and wide
To see poor Fred, Kentucky fried.   *Margaret Whitelegg*

As Jack bent to retrieve his hat,
A truck drove by and squashed him flat.
Remarked his grieving widow, Flora,
"At least it missed his new fedora."

When Joe ran to the liquor store
His heart gave out. He lived no more.
His wife said to their son, young Fred,
"Can you bring home the booze instead?"

Carole Vaughan

"Justice!" Ellen's lawyer cried,
"Her Coke contained formaldehyde!"
But judgment had to be reserved;
She seemed so awfully well preserved. *Russell Wodell*

My wife, expecting in the fall,
Consumed an India rubber ball.
When questioned, she explained, "Now maybe
I shall have a bouncing baby." *Mike Snipper*

My dog was dying by the inch.
To die by the inch is hard.
So I took him out in the alley,
And let him die by the yard.   *Dave Lindsay*

The parents ordered steak flambé.
The flames engulfed their daughter.
The waiter doused her with a spray
And charged them for the water.   *Tony Chandler*

Mr. Jones, while pruning his apple tree,
Fell from a branch and injured his knee.
He inspected the limb and with scarcely a pause
Just trimmed it off with one of his saws.   *Margaret Burden*

Sweet Sally May blew her husband away
And met with her lawyer the very same day.
She showed no remorse, nor a sorrowful look,
As they talked about rights for the film and the book.
                                             Wendy Goldenson

While skiing on a season's pass,
John vanished in a deep crevasse.
I hope they find him in the snow;
His pass has got three months to go.   *Arthur M. Lipman*

Daily, Robert swam the moat
Until he met the king's new boat.
Said the tearful captain, on the shore:
"Alas, we'll see him, Bob, no more."   *M. Thompson*

My periodontist, Dr. Moss,
Insists that I forever floss.
Now, although no tartar lingers,
I've lost the ends of all my fingers.

Pa, a-weary of the chirrup,
Lined the aviary with syrup:
Not so much, he said, to mute 'em;
Rather, easier to shoot 'em.

Printshop Pete, to cure his dolours,
Pushed his boss between the rollers;
The boss, pressed for his views, said, "I'll
Straighten out *Your* Morning Smile."   *Jim Parr*

My wife committed suicide,
Yet I am nothing daunted.
I charge admission where she died,
For now the place is haunted.   *C.S. Williams*

The arsenic was in the milk.
The drink slipped down as smooth as silk.
The heirs, in death-row cells, ask how
The cops had failed to charge the cow.   *Shelagh Peever*

Mythical Places

The challenge, courtesy of Jack Mansell, was to place a mythical town in an existing province, territory or state. I took a lenient attitude toward abbreviations, particularly since the United States has just finished altering a good many of them.

Trots, Ky.
Oompa, Pa.   *Jack Orbaum*

Pi, Que.   *Jack Waserman*

Bon, Mo.
Swift Current, D.C.   *Michael Thomas*

Olive, Me.   *Howard Barrett*

Boderek, Tenn.
Ominepaw, Pa.
Miscella, N.Y.   *Mike England*

Mine Closed, Oregon.
Waitasec, Alaska.   *Brian Yamashita*

Lo, Cal.
Tragic, Fla. *June Martin*

Yorrick, Alas.
Lay, Tex. *John Borthwick*

Ça, Va. *Alan McNairn*

Cheer, IO.
Egg, Wisc.
Pean, UT.
Oh, OH. *Ruth Ann Pepall*

Uncle, Ont.
Lepre, Conn. *Lois Schroeder Loewen*

Huwatwenwer, Wy.
Wait, N.C. *David Rotenberg*

Eh, B.C. *Tony and Jennifer Chandler*

Muslim, Calif. *Eusebio L. Koh*

Underlocken, Ky.
Disemb, Ark.
Pop, N.J.   *Charles Crockford*

Dingdong, Del.
Stic, Ky.   *Elizabeth Quance*

Yo Yo, MA.   *Martha Keaner*

Outfield, Nfld.
Palm, PEI.
Emmeneau, P.Q.
Carr, MA.   *Anton Kuerti*

Oola, La.
Hoot, Mon.   *Lois J. Grant*

Doremifaso, La.   *Les Holroyd*

Fyvan, Tenn.   *Georgina Evans Johns*

Nowhere, Man.
Singalong, Mich.
Corned Beef, RI.
Penis, NV.   *Jim Ballinger*

Eyeof, NWT.
Truf, FL.   *Gloria Ellenton*

Larry Curly, Mo.   *Suzy Tanzer*

Pie Mode, Ala.   *M. Thompson*

Human, Ariz.   *Tina Bauer*

Ego, ID.	*Charles Anthony Stuart*
Oldencran, Ky.	*Michael Davies*
Ms., Miss.	*Al Wilkinson*
No Question, Sask. Plume de Mat, Ont.	*Andrew Allentuck*
Eeyi-Eeyi, OH.	*W. Appel*
Hippopota, Mass. Luna, TX.	*Juliet Janes*
Praise, Ala.	*June Skene*
Magnum, PEI. Yes, Virginia.	*Ed Kamps*
Gee, Wis. Pudd, Del.	*Craig Cole*
Sept-huit, Newf.	*K.C. Angus*
Amorphous, Mass.	*Alanna Little*

New Orders of Canada

This was the second Challenge set, on Feb. 9, 1991:
Invent a fourth Order of Canada, for Canadians unlikely
to receive one of the first three, and list the qualifications.
For the record, the first three are Companion, Officer and
Member. Holding one of those honours already is no bar
to receiving one of the following.

Whiner of the Order of Canada

Awarded for contributions to Canadian unity by
persistent attacks on permanent institutions such as
the Queen, the United States, bilingualism,
monolingualism, capitalism, socialism, Ontario,
Quebec, history, geography, etc.　　　　　*A.G. Rigg*

Nerd of the Order of Canada

Conferred upon persons who have contributed little
or nothing to Canada and are appointed to protect
the Order against accusations of elitism.

David Mayerovitch

Disorder of Canada

This rare individual resists all pressure to maintain his house and garden in an attractive manner. His overgrown lawn, unweeded garden, mossy roof, peeling paint and precariously tilting fence all combine to create feelings of superiority in his otherwise ordinary neighbours. Provides topic of conversation for neighbours who otherwise have little to say to each other. Caution: Notice of award ceremony may get lost among junk mail.

Virginia Hayes

The Order of Canada, Creative Procrastination

Presented to Mr. Rupert Laidback for his contribution to past and current policies of Government, High Finance and Church Synods. His theory is as follows: "Any item of business shall be referred to an appointed Committee, said Committee to report back in six months. Said Committee also has the power to appoint a Task Force which will in turn report back to the Committee in a further six months. At the end of that time the item of business will no longer be relevant, and can be dismissed."

Gerry MacIntosh

member of the disorder of canada

Pontificator of the Order of Canada
Awarded to those opinionated orators who delight
in pronouncing precisely how they (as opposed to
the person in power) would do something, only
when (a) they are highly unlikely ever to be in a position where they could implement their plan, and
(b) they would never suffer from any of the plan's
unmentioned side-effects. Particular distinction is
due those who pontificate in fields for which they
have no conceivable expertise or professional qualifications.   *M.J. Armstrong*

Who Dat? of the Order of Canada
The recipient must exemplify the one quality for
which Canadians are famous, and as such must be
able to be the only person in a room and not be noticed. He/she will not have been heard of before receiving the award, and, after getting it, will not be
heard of again. The person presenting the award
usually arrives fifteen minutes late, and mispro-
nounces the recipient's name.   *Charles Crockford*

Janus of the Order of Canada
To be awarded to that bland, smiling, verbose public servant who made two contradictory promises,
believed them both himself and saw no difficulty in
implementing both at the same time.   *Don Suthers*

Imaginary Sequels

*The challenge, which came from colleague Andrew
Coyne, was to suggest book or play sequels that might
have been. A couple of readers suggested The Globe and
E-Mail.*

The Wizard of Lb.   *A. Taylor*

The Chardonnay of Wrath.   *Eric Hurowitz*

II, Claudius.
The Communist Bill of Lading.   *Arthur Andrew*

The Used Testament.
Sophie's Second Choice.   *Charles Templeton*

A Long History of Time: The Unabridged Version.
                          Nancy and Michael Parke-Taylor

An Aftertaste of Honey.   *Heather Peacock*

Snow White and Her Seventh Divorce.
Erica Jong's Fear of Landing.   *Helen and Paul McCusker*

Richard II, II.
The Greatest Story Ever Retold.
You Can't Go Home Again, Again.   *Glenda Bocknek*

The Concrete Jungle Book.
As For Me and My Monster House.
Zen and the Art of Rollerblade Maintenance.

Roger Cullman

Portnoy's Refund.   *R.G. MacNeill*

The Firmer (to be followed by: The Firmest).

Bryan Ferguson

Pierre Berton's The Last Train.   *David B. Clipsham*

Wuthered Heights.   *Simon Brodie*

The Scarlet Letter: B.   *Susan Lichtblau*

Snow White and Prince Charming: An Unauthorized
Biography.   *Joe Silva*

Bald (sequel to Hair).
Generation X + 1.   *Fred Farr*

Frankenstein: The Missing Parts.   *Brian Cameron*

The Tibetan Book of the Resurrected.   *Candy Pattenick*

The Cacophony of the Sheep.   *Tom Deeprose and friends*

Old Possum's Book of Litters.   *Rose Baines Dyson*

Just So-So Stories.   *Peter Herbert*

Endofmarch.   *Marni Cappe*

The Evenyssey.   *K.C. Angus*

Who Else is Afraid of Virginia Woolf?   *Cy Steele*

The Arrival of Godot.
The Conciser Ox Diksh.   *John Sullivan*

The Pickwick Faxes.
Anne of Green Gables Comes Out.
Hamlet, Prince of the European Community.
                                        David Mayerovitch

The Video of Kells.   *Helen and Peter Marucci*

H.G. Wells' The Overtime Machine.   *Phil Gurski*

Sunshine Sketches of a Metropolitan Urban Area.
Winston the Pooh, Investment Banker.

Alison Cunningham

The Ugly Duckling à l'Orange. *Maureen Korman*

The Neverending Neverending Story. *Sandra Lloyd*

Jude the Famous. *Ian Guthrie*

Debrett's Steerage. *Bill Alexander*

The Water Babies in Junior High. *R.M. Baxter*

The Man Who Was Friday. *Jim Parr*

A.A. Milne's Now We Are Seventy-Six.
Pauline Johnson's The Song My Inboard-Outboard
   Lower Unit Sings. *Leslie Tomlinson*

Apocalypse Now and Again.
Dracula Revamped. *J. Simandl and Henry Ko*

Malcolm Y. *Mary Anne Rubin*

Lord Chatterley's Implant. *Philip Thornhill*

The Poseidon Royal Commission. *Lois J. Halls*

Dickens' Nicholas Dimeby. *Vern and Eleanor Gilbert*

The Next World According to Garp.
Eugene Twogin.
Cretaceous Park.
The Ultrasound of Music.   *Sue Dulley*

Frank Herbert's Dune to Death.   *J. Lipkovits*

Leonard Cohen's The Favourite Game, Tournament
   Edition.   *David Frank*

A Child's Boxing Day in Wales.   *Arthur Loughton*

Rosemary's Tubal Ligation.
The Skin of Our Dentures.   *John Bishopric*

Jurassic Double-Park.   *Delia Schoor*

I Am a Camcorder.
The Iceman Melteth.
The Niebelungen Ring Twice.   *Helen and Eugene Strauss*

An Encore by the Alexandria Quartet.
I Am a Camera: New Developments.
The RePeter Principle.   *Ken Purvis*

Hair II: The Transplant.
Blade Walker.   *Colin McGuire*

Carousel: The Spinoff.
Sweeney Todd: Another Close Shave.   *Cherry Watson*

Red Riding Hood Framed Me: The Wolf's Story.
                                            Yvonne Knight

Pushing the Button

The challenge, suggested by Edward G. Pleva, was to explain the purpose of the number-sign button (#) on the touch-tone phone. It might, for instance, be for tiny games of tictactoe while your call is on hold.

Where the angels who dance on the head of a pin do their floor exercises.

Also a space symbol, it acknowledges the twilight zone in which forgotten callers linger, trying to remember who they were phoning and why in the first place.

For important decision-makers to consult their numerologists.

Also a music symbol, it permits callers to hear a little melody while being reminded occasionally that "your call is important to us."   *Alanna Little*

Free-trade button that converts U.S. measurements to
metric, and vice versa, during cross-border
conversations.

Leaves a painful "#" brand on your fingertip, as a
reminder that you shouldn't mess with things you
don't understand.

Digitally distorts the voices of callers for your
entertainment (e.g. can make your mother-in-law
sound like Donald Duck).

Responds to obscene calls with the recorded message:
"You are now being transferred to our call-tracing
department. One moment, please..."

Converts your telephone into a calculator,
multi-function watch and video game.

Alerts the phone company that you are fooling with
their equipment and triggers a threatening call from
Ernestine the Operator.   *Al Wilkinson*

The internationally recognized reminder of the
number of precious minutes wasted on a
meaningless call.   *Conrad J. McCallum*

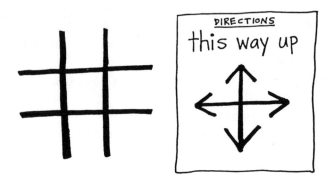

Enables an optometrist to give an over-the-telephone
eye exam: "Look to the bottom right of your
telephone. Close your left eye. Are the vertical or
horizontal lines darker?" *Jim Kullman*

To comfort inebriated bar patrons who are calling
taxis; even if they dial while standing on their
heads, the symbol looks the same. *Charles Crockford*

The "#" represents cross-purposes, a symbol for
Canada. *David Savage*

To swear gently when you reach an answering
machine, as in !*@#! *David Nimmo*

The Shift Mode on your touch-tone telephone enables
you to dial the letters instead of the numbers.
A.G. Rigg

The designers thought they were asked to make a
phone with 11 number buttons, which they did.
When it was discovered they needed only 10, they
scratched out the number 11 with two horizontal
lines. *George Kraemer*

Little-known Last Words

The challenge was to devise famous last words that well-known figures might have spoken on their deathbed. As an example, I gave Abraham Lincoln saying, "Now I'll never know how it ends." Albert Furtwangler of Sackville, N.B., responded with a note: "The Challenge example was about Lincoln not getting to see the end of the play at Ford's Theatre. You may be interested to know that no one saw the end of that performance and the theatre was closed permanently. I happen to have written a book on the subject: Assassin on Stage: Brutus, Hamlet and the Death of Lincoln."

Nostradamus: "Well, this comes as no surprise."
Alexander Graham Bell: "Hold my calls."
Socrates: "Does this taste funny, or is it just me?"

Michael J. Gilbert

Amelia Earhart: "Oh, oh. Did those guys at the
   airport say gallons or litres?"   *S. Muench*

Sigmund Freud: "I'm slipping away."
Elvis Presley: "Return to sender."
Humpty Dumpty: "Does anyone have some
    Superglue?"
Mae West: "Come up or down and see me some
    time."
Clint Eastwood: "Make my afterlife."   *Glenn Patterson*

Mackenzie King: "Coming, Mother."   *Jack Orbaum*

W.C. Fields: "I would like another bier."
                                    Peter B. Watkins

Eva Braun: "This is a heck of a way to spend a
    honeymoon."   *Barry Mallard*

Marshall McLuhan: "From now on, the medium will
    be my message."   *Larry Sianchuk*

Fred Astaire: "The jig is up."
Harry Houdini: "Now watch closely!"
Oscar Wilde: "I'm at wit's end."
Arturo Toscanini: "No more rehearsals."
                                    Albert Furtwangler

Methusaleh: "I never did get my old-age pension."

George F. Rogers

Samuel Pepys: "No more peeps." *Freda K. Thomas*

Alfred Hitchcock: "Now fade to black."
H.J. Heinz: "Variety 58 was just about ready for the
    market." *Les Holroyd*

Edsel Ford: "Do you think I'll be recalled?"
Thomas Edison: "Are the lights dimming, dear?"

James Nichols

Joan of Arc: "A little rain wouldn't do any harm."
Mackenzie King: "WALKIES!"
Charles Dickens: "Please, sir, can I have some ... "

Stuart Alcock

Captain of the Titanic: "Who put that there?"
King Tut: "Hey guys ... Guys!!!" *Tony Miller*

Joan of Arc: "My last meal is a marshmallow on a
    stick?" *Ron Padgett*

Ambivalent References

Suppose that somebody applying for a job asks you to write a letter of recommendation, but you consider the person incompetent or worse. How do you draft your letter in a way that, while positive, reflects a certain ambivalence? This challenge, suggested by Chris Galea of Toronto, touched a responsive chord among readers, many of whom had done it for real.

"Having seen the applicant at work, I would recommend that you waste no time in hiring him."

Alan E. Devine

"No words can describe adequately her contribution to our firm. Hard work is the least of her abilities."
"His departure will have an immediate effect on the firm's productivity."

Colin Fleming

"There is no saying what he is capable of. His new
filing system turned this company around."

Dale Scaife

"Knowing the quality of his work as I do, it is my
pleasure to surrender his services to you."

Agnes Stewart

"I am pleased to recommend Mr. Jones, whom I am
sure you will find a promising young man."

Terence Campbell

"You need waste no time training him in the use of
the photocopier, fax machine or telephone system;
he will make a quick study of them himself."
"We have found him to be an exceptionally
independent and innovative thinker, an individual
who seems never to be restrained by the rigidity of
schedules, formats or procedure." *Jennifer Duholke*

"This businessman's record with the 23 companies
where he has been previously employed should
speak for itself." *Philippa Hunter*

"I can guarantee that if you hire Charlie, every day
  will become a day to remember as he strives to
  meet your demands." *Eric Adams*

"Once I realized Mr. Smith's actual qualifications
  and capabilities, he never disappointed me." *Paul Bell*

"He lived up to our expectations. His going prolongs
  a vacuum in our work force." *Zita Cameron*

"She will never be caught shirking, does not know the
  meaning of the words 'sick leave' and is
  unperturbed by the prospect of frequent turnover
  among her subordinates." *Jane Wangersky*

"His ability to foster and develop interpersonal
  relationships in an office environment truly marks
  him as an *homme d'affaires*."
"I am at a loss to describe his loyalty, industry and
  dedication. In this I am most sincere." *Frank Haigh*

"Mr. Smith has been with us for 15 years. There will
  be no replacing him."
"You will miss his presence, as I have, on those days
  when he isn't in." *N.J. Asrican*

"He is one of a few truly creative accountants we
  have employed. As you know, most of them put
  two and two together and get four, whereas he has
  taken us one step beyond that concept." *Tony Rother*

"In my business, I have had the pleasure of working
with many outstanding people. Today, I write to
you about John Doe."
"Should you choose him to manage your business,
you may never need anyone else." *Dan Tisch*

"I am delighted to hear that he has applied for a job
with you, one of our foremost competitors."
Morton S. Rapp

"Her articles for our magazine always incorporated
the works of the world's finest writers." *Alanna Little*

"I have never known him to do anything he was not
told." *Andrew Macpherson*

"He is a progressive loans manager who
courageously expanded the bank's clientele."
Al Wilkinson

"I cannot honestly say enough about this lady's
personal qualifications."
"This man's conviction will serve the best interests of
your business." *Don Suthers*

"Knowing that you have already recruited 11 people
for your 12-man crew, Joe is certainly the last
person I would recommend."
"As a pharmacist, John dispenses with care."
Michael H. Orr

"He can be counted on to do a good job when dealing
with matters he considers important." *Ralph M. Logan*

"Mr. Smith's relations with his fellow workers are
unique. Many lack the cultural background to
appreciate his offbeat and raucous sense of
humour. A positive result is that Mr. Smith's
favourite place in the office, the water cooler, is
free of gossiping employees." *Charles Bastomsky*

"I can safely say that you will not be troubled by his
absenteeism." *Steven Rosenhek*

"We have never had an employee like Max. Once he
starts a job he just doesn't quit. We wish more
employees could be fired with such enthusiasm."
Ann Timonin

"He has an inquisitive nature. He never tires of asking
questions of his supervisors."
"You won't catch him napping. He always appears to
have his nose to the grindstone." *Brian Yamashita*

"Meeting deadlines is never a worry with him."
Carolyn Joyce Brown

Franchises to Avoid

The challenge was to provide examples of franchises that investors would be wise to avoid. This one was suggested by the Crawford, Galea and Merry families, working together as a team, whose examples included Kentucky Fried Liver and The Dead Body Shop.

One Step Ahead law offices
No Pain, No Gain dental centres   *Dennis Skalko*

Squint Optical
Mañana Auto Glass
Rocky Reef Vacation Cruises
Big Bang Muffler Services
Lethargy Car Wash   *Eric Adams*

Stiffs 'R' Us funeral homes   *M. Keats*

Radioactive Shack   *G. Norton-Wilks*

McPemmican   *Wendy McDonald*

U-Drill-It dental clinics
Slug-on-a-Stick   *Stuart McDonald*

Pied Piper of Hamelin day-care centres
Titanic Holiday Cruises
Canadian Seckretarial Schools   *Peter Marucci*

Mind Your Own Business Consultants   *Joan Bond*

London Fog Optical   *Ralph Strong*

Vlad's for Steaks   *D.C. Ellwood*

Miss Anthrope's Introduction Service
Suckers and Nuts Confectionery   *Ruth Brown*

Boiled Cabbage on a Stick   *Timothy Wild*

Night Flight Investors
Ecocidal Shampoo   *John Ferguson*

Leaky's Radiator Service
Windy's restaurants   *Ed Kamps*

Kidney Delight
Herring Hut   *Rob McMenemy*

The English-Language Sign Co., Montreal Division
Happiness Tissue-Paper Condoms
Ontario Zebra Mussels Farms, Inc.   *Charles Crockford*

Golden Gristle restaurants   *Blair Ferguson*

International House of Tripe
Icarus Flying School
Hannibal Lecter's Food Emporium   *Brendan J. O'Byrne*

Sam the Wax Cylinder Man   *Mack Furlong*

Diana's Sweetbreads
Radio Shock: "You are our quality control!"
The Bates Journey's End Motel   *G. Helge Koch*

Eureka Perfumes
Ella's Salmon
Rorschach Printing   *Charles K. Long*

Maison Cheval Gourmet Restaurant   *Al Wilkinson*

Fractured French

In his book Fractured French Encore, Ormonde de Kay offered unusual English translations of common French expressions. Example: tour de force (obligatory sightseeing). Uncertain whether I was cementing national unity or destroying it, I invited readers to provide their own examples.

Fin de siècle: A frozen shark delicacy.
Raison d'être: The only justification for eating bran
  flakes.   *Eva Hecht*

Fait accompli: Quality Greek cheese.
Rive gauche: A vulgar alderman.   *Allan Gould*

Faute de mieux: Cat with laryngitis.
Pièce de résistance: Uncompleted jigsaw puzzle.
Roman à clef: Imprisoned Italian.   *Lynn Gold*

La vie en rose: The kiddies' bathroom is pink.
Maison chic: Hen-house. *Joan Lea*

Tout à l'heure: Wake-up call. *Margaret Toth*

Comme ci, comme ça: Parisian playground equipment.
John Summers

Bon mot: One of the Three Stooges. *Paul Savard*

Laissez-faire: Dog show for collies. *Halliday family*

Pour rire: All deliveries at the back door, please.
Sang froid: Not much warmth in her voice.
Salle à manger: Messy eater. *Arthur M. Lipman*

Sans souci: No raw fish, please.
Tant pis, tant mieux: My aunt has washed her hands;
   her sense of angst has been assuaged.
À bras ouverts: Honestly, you think they'd have *some*
   sense of shame! *R.R. Jeffels*

Entente cordial: Happy campers.
Poste restante: Canada Post.
Défense de cracher: Safety barrier.
Cordon bleu: Police barricade.
Clair de lune: Spent my last dollar.
Vin ordinaire: Unmarked police car.

Ray and Jo Haythornthwaite

Char à banc: Joint account. *Irma Coucill*

Tout ensemble: Horn section. *Eusebio L. Koh*

Pousse-café: Cat restaurant. *Maria J. Bell*

Filet mignon: A female Shetland pony. *James A. Garrett*

De temps en temps: Unstable office situation.

Martha Keaner

Cul de sac: Removal of extraneous articles from your
purse. *Jean Lehman*

Sans souci: Suzie's lost. *Genevieve Moreau*

Hors d'oeuvre: Outside worker. *H. Metszies*

Mot juste: Please wait a moment.
Bête noire: Elizabeth returned from Florida with an
excellent tan. *Jean Lehman*

Eau de citron: Car loan unpaid. *Edward H. Thring*

Too Many Cookbooks

Since cookbooks generally outsell other books, it seemed only fair to give the others a fighting chance by altering the titles to appeal to the cookbook market. The entries flooded in, with many suggesting The Right Stuffing, War and Pizza, Lady Chatterley's Liver, Alice Through the Cooking Class and Northrop Frye's The Great Cod.

Yeast of Edam.
Wuthering Haggis.
Brunch Over the River Kwai.
Tortillas in the Mist.
Tequila Mockingbird.
Ivancoho.
The Kama Sushi.
Crepes of Wrath.

Ozzie's Restaurant staff

The Barbecue of Seville.

Jack Orbaum

Never Fry Wolf.
Pickwick Peppers.
To Grill a Mockingbird.   *Maria Bell*

Decline and Fall of the Romaine Empire.
The Book of Common Bear.
The Pear, Yes Sir!
A Hare for Owen Meany.   *Allan Gould*

Trout of Africa.
Gorky Pork.   *Jenipher Mackenzie*

The Clan of the Camembert.
Rumproast of the Bailey.   *Earl Liu*

Torte d'Arthur.   *Terry Rodgers*

A Clockwork Duck à l'Orange.
Teas of the d'Urbervilles.   *Chris Robson*

Even Cowgirls Get the Blueberries.
War and Peach.
Gone With the Wine.   *Susan Cochrane*

crepes of wrath

Pride and Prune Juice.
The Anchovy and the Ecstasy.
Jonathan Livingston Seafood.   *E.M. MacNeil*

The Unbearable Rightness of Beans.
Tart of Darkness.
Bonfire of the Canapés.   *Celine Papizewska*

The Handmaid's Tamale.
Twelfth Nightcap.   *Richard Berzaitis*

The Engineer of Humid Rolls.
The Incomparable Haddock.
As For Me and My Grouse.
The Satanic Perches.   *Johanna Preston*

Anise in Wonderland.
Jacob Tofu and the Hooded Fang.   *Brink family*

Rice and Fowl of the Third Reich.   *Charles Lambie*

The Lunch Bag of Notre Dame.
The Fritter of Wakefield.   *David Savage*

The Stone-Wheat Angel.
Cooking for Mr. Goodbar.
Fiddleheads on the Roof.
2001: A Spice Odyssey.
Huckleberry Muffin.
The Pepper-Mill on the Floss.
Liver to Heaven.   *Glenda Bocknek*

As I Lay Dieting.
The Salad of the Bad Café.   *Christopher Levenson*

Robinson Croissant.
Of Maize and Men.
How Clean Was My Galley.
King Solomon's Minestrone.   *Kenneth Garner*

A Streetcar Named Dessert.
Last Mango in Paris.   *Frances Tessier*

Pita Pan.
As You Lick It.   *Maureen Richardson*

Lord of the Onion Rings.
Origin of Spices.   *Colleen Livingstone*

Fish Business.
The Rhubarbyat of Omar Cayenne.
In the Peanut Colony.
The Tempura of Our Times.   *Susan Kent and Rik Davidson*

Oregano of Species.
Perogy and Bess.
The Last Pike.
The Prime Rib of Miss Jean Brodie.   *Martin Penner*

The Seven Pilafs of Wisdom.
A Quiche Before Dying.
A Christmas Carrot.   *Peter Warren*

The Pound Cake of the Baskervilles.   *John Borthwick*

The Dairy of Samuel Pepys.
Wine in the Willows.   *B.E. Organ*

The Scarlet Lettuce.   *Oonagh Barry*

Squidnapped.
The Old Curiosity Chop. *Judy Cornwell*

Anchovy Adverse.
Beef Encounter.
Come Back Little Sherbet. *John McPhee*

The Pita and the Pappadum.
Remembrance of Things Pasta.
The Mayo of Casterbridge.
Twenty Thousand Leeks Under the Sea. *Robert Smith*

Pilgrim's Produce. *Sandy Winsby*

Voltaire's Candied. *María-Elena Déry*

Julia Child's Christmas in Wales. *Sheilagh Geer*

The Old Man and the Brie.
Much Ragout About Nothing. *Diane Bethune*

The Goulash Archipelago. *Elizabeth Macpherson*

Critique of Pure Raisin.
Das Kanapes.
Kirsch-22. *Colin McLaren*

A Sausage to India. *Vera Cooke*

Eats of Eden.
Lox Horizon. *Samm MacKay*

Breakfast of Champignons. *Mark Svensson*

One Hundred Years of Solid Food.   *D.M. Brooker*

The Red Batch of Curry.
The Pitcher of Dorian Gravy.
Truffles With My Aunt.   *Richard W. Lawton*

Out of Paprika.
Tenderize the Night.
Murder on the Orient Espresso.   *Mike Snipper*

Peter Pancake.
Barnaby Fudge.   *Lesley P. Lyon*

Bran of Green Gables.   *Mary-Ann Archibald*

Lady Chatterley's Larder.
The Bonbons of the Vanities.   *Alan Cantor and Leslie Gotfut*

Adventures of Tom Soya.   *Jessica Olshen*

The New Taste o' Mint.
The Gizzard of Oz.   *Luis Cabeza*

The Ancient Marinade.   *Tony Chandler*

A Brief History of Thyme.   *Jennifer Chandler*

Cress of the d'Urbervilles.   *Barbara Middleton*

The Joy Luck Club Sandwich.
One Flew Over the Bird's Nest Soup.   *Cynthia Martin*

A Confederacy of Doughnuts.
Thus Baked Zarathustra.   *Tim Falconer*

Uncle Tom's Cabbage.   *Tom & Fiona Gunn*

Cry Haddock!
Thomas Carlyle's French Revolution, or How to Use
    a Moulinex.   *Ernle Chatfield*

The Complete Woks of Shakespeare.   *Diane Kemp*

Who Has Seen the Wiener?
Tarragon With the Wind.
My Brother's Kipper.
Catsup-22.   *Phyllis Daly*

The Prince and the Pepper.
A Tale of Two Satays.
The Pita Principle.
Tandoori is the Night.
The Flan of the Cave Bear.   *Eric Vernon*

Braise the Titanic!
Love in the Time of Cholesterol.
I Heard the Bowl Call My Name.   *David Dunsmuir*

Tom Swifties

There must be something in the Tom Swifty that touches a nation's soul, horrible as that is to contemplate. I was swamped by hundreds of triple entendres and excruciating puns, the more bearable of which are included here. The Tom Swifty is named after Tom Swift, the hero of the series of boy's-own science adventures by Victor Appleton. Appleton had an inordinate fondness for adverbs, usually redundant, and certainly without the double meanings that the parlour game introduced.

"I've lost my dog," said Dagwood lackadaisically.
"I wish Bonanza would return to TV," said Tom
    forlornly.   *Paul Hibbert*

"I'll take the prisoner downstairs," he said
    condescendingly.
"I can *so* recite Paradise Lost backwards," he said
    controversially.
"I think I left my Hesperus poem in the bar," said
    Longfellow recklessly.   *Richard W. Lawton*

"This must be the right lake," Champlain said eerily.
                                 Ulrich Kretschmar

"I'll never feed the crocodiles again," said Captain
Hook offhandedly. *John McGuinness*

"I feel like Chinese soup tonight," she said wantonly.
Betty Stackhouse

"My skirt isn't clinging to my stockings!" she said
ecstatically. *Blair Holtam*

"This is very good bouillabaisse," she said
superficially. *Pauline Moyd*

"Let's blast off from the moon," said the astronaut
apologetically.
"Some large animals spend too much time in the
water," said the rhinoceros hypocritically.
"Who set fire to pussy?" he asked catalytically.
"On his death bed he renounced the church," said the
doctor diagnostically. *Tim and Sheila Andrew*

"I wish I could afford that European car," she sighed
audibly. *Helga Wachsmuth*

..he said disparately...

"Via Rail doesn't travel here any more," he said
extraneously.   *Warren Ford*

"The bird died," he said disparately.   *Wayne Harvey*

"Where is the Champs Elysees?" he asked ruefully.
                                                  Bill Carroll

"Meow!" remarked Sylvester chattily.   *Wallace McLeod*

"Try this new feline medicine," said the vet
catatonically.   *Roxane Ward*

"Garlic is good for what ails you," said Tom
bilingually.   *Warren Stevenson*

"I fooled Mr. Price," he said convincingly.   *Bruce Rusk*

"Guess where I'm taking you for dinner," she said
archly.
"John, I hear something moving out by the
campfire," she whispered intently.   *Catherine McVicar*

"Help, I'm trapped in the Wizard's necklace," Tom
said independently.   *Stephen Hart*

"I can't stand Hamlet," said Tom disdainfully.
                                               Lester Peterson

"I have *not* been cheating on my diet," he said piously.
                                                  Ted Arnold

Traffic Signs

Perhaps it was the harrowing experience of driving in Montreal and Toronto that made me wonder whether Canada needed a new series of traffic signs, such as "No left turn from right lane," or "Dim headlights, if working." Readers were invited to submit their own versions.

Ben Barkow recalled a sign he saw mounted on New York bridges in the 1960s: In case of air raid, drive off bridge. "There's nothing wrong in principle with this sign. It's just that driving off a bridge means something different than simply 'proceed to end of bridge.' Perhaps it's there to counteract the natural urge to watch an atomic bomb explode over Manhattan from the bridge."

Yield to vehicles reversing out of driveways.
Four-way stop sign ahead: Avoid eye contact.

H. Metszies

Blow horn during U-turns, 4-6 p.m.
Pedestrians, use green at own risk.
Red-light running: five-car limit.
Cyclists: 30 km/h limit on sidewalk.

Eric Adams

Welcome to Ontario: Signalling lane changes
  prohibited.
Paved shoulder driving permitted if late for work.

Larry Doyle

Speed bumps: Slower traffic keep right.   *Ken Lum*

Exit right for gas: free estimates, loans and mortgages
  arranged.
Pedestrian crossing: Slow to 90 km/h.
Amber light ahead: Increase speed.   *Ron Jeffels*

No U-turn on one-way street.   *E.D. Martyr*

Unlawful to tailgate for purpose of reading
  personalized licence plates.   *Charles Crockford*

Curves ahead: hands-free cellular only.
Entering Toronto city limits: Hazardous road
  conditions next 20 miles.
No standing (rush hours excepted).   *Lloyd Nesbitt*

One parking place per vehicle.   *G.A. Taylor*

Turn signal not required unless turning. *P. Froislie*

Traffic circle: Close eyes and pray.
Hector McNeill and Lois Anderson

Maximum 100: minimum 120.
No right turn, 7-9 a.m., Mon-Fri, unless you want to
turn right. *Al Forest*

If the green colour of this light is not suitable, you are
under no obligation to move.
Use of turn signals is optional at speeds greater than
50 km/h.
Cyclists must pass on the right when approaching a
vehicle in the right-turn lane. *Craig Dellio*

Welcome to Sudbury. Posted speed limits are for
information only. *B.E. Organ*

Pedestrians: Caution, do not cross if light is red,
amber or green. *Gord Brannen*

Slow drivers use passing lane. *Eric Bundock*

Watch for oncoming traffic when driving on left of
centre line.
Winding road: Do not apply lipstick. *Tony Chandler*

First and Last Date

Ah, romance. The challenge was to suggest ways you can tell that a first date isn't working out. Lisa Richards summed up the thoughts of many entrants: "Wow! What a challenge it is to recapture all those rendezvous blues!"

You're parked in her driveway, and she looks at you
and says, "Do I have a girl for you!"   *Charles Crockford*

She starts your first evening with the words, "If
you're an Aquarius, I'd rather call it quits right
now."
He starts the evening off with, "I've got this
superstition thing — no movies or shows with an A
in the title."   *Eric Adams*

While at his apartment for a pre-dinner drink, you
peek into his bedroom and find the walls plastered
with provocative pinups — all male.   *Maria J. Bell*

He takes you to a restaurant and offers you the chair
with the obvious food stains on it.

He says he'll order for both of you, then selects the
cheapest items on the menu.

After five minutes of conversation, he says he doesn't
want to get involved.

When discussing world politics, he says Adolf Hitler
was basically a misunderstood prophet.

He seems to know just a little *too* much about robbing
a bank.

He questions you constantly about your knockout
roommate.

He says he has recently begun to question his sexual
orientation.

As the meal arrives, he takes the gum out of his
mouth and sticks it under the table.

He tells you he doesn't believe in using silverware.

His idea of a fun mealtime activity is "chew and
show."   *Dianne Daminoff and Lisa Richards*

When he escorts you to his car, you find his mother
sitting in the back seat.   *Morton S. Rapp*

He keeps running out to put nickels in the parking
    meter.
                                Lily Silver

At the movie, he holds hands with the girl on the
    other side of him.
From his mezzanine seats at the symphony, she
    points out the front-orchestra location where she
    sat last week with another date.
He presents her with flowers which she realizes were
    plucked from her neighbour's front garden.
                                Alanna Little

"That was a wonderful evening, Pete," and his name
    is John.
"I'm going to be a priest."
"I hope you don't mind sitting in the back seat, the
    dog is used to riding in front."
"I like to practice my bagpipes when the house is
    quiet."
"I feel we should wear gloves until we get to know
    each other better."
                              H. Metszies

He orders a bowl of water for his invisible dog.
He sends back the gazpacho soup because it's cold.
He tells you his friends call him "Captain Adventure."
You notice he holds his fork in his fist.   *Josie Stankiewicz*

TV or not TV

Would TV shows improve if they were inspired by works of great literature? Readers were asked to provide synopses for this brave new world of programming. E.g. Oh, Those Brothers Karamazov!: Ivan has trouble with his soul again.

My Favourite La Manchan: Sancho tries to interest his boss in reality therapy.

Offred!: The Commander's wife encourages Offred to start dating other men.

Littleuns' Island: The boys work hard on plans for a barbecue. Ralph, though, has other ideas.

David and Kathleen Dunsmuir

Le Sport d'Arthur: Arthur spends his days with Pellinore, charging after the Questing Beast, unaware of Gwen's temptation back at the castle. Lance struggles with his conscience, but loses.

Slingin' in the Thanes: Lady Macbeth strives to reverse her sagging fortunes by gathering the thanes for a bumptious banquet. Her domestic ambitions are thwarted, however, by a stubborn red stain that just won't go away.

Patricia Smith

Great Expectations Again: Pip, learning that his
benefactor Magwitch is wanted by the police,
dresses him in women's clothes and passes him off
as Miss Havisham's sister. But Estella pays him a
surprise visit!
Crusoe and Company: Rob gives up on the idea of
building a raft from dead fish. Friday hurts his back
while practicing the minuet in his hammock.
Moby and the Captain: Ahab sees red when he
discovers that his peg leg has termites! Meanwhile,
Moby decides to ram the Captain's boat just for fun.
The Ringer of Notre Dame: Quasimodo is depressed
when the cardinals turn down his request for a loan
to open a school for bell-ringers. Meanwhile, there
are bats where he tolls!   *Garry Ferrier*

My Three Sons: Nosy neighbours heckle as Noah and
his boys build a boat in the back yard.
I Love Gertrude. Wacky hijinks ensue when old
Uncle Claudius has a crush on Hamlet's mom.
                                        Edgar D. Slater

mr. noah's neighbourhood

Iliad Blues: Helen finally gets to see Paris, but not in
the way she anticipated.

Ali Baba and the Fortysomething Thieves: Ali and
his friends re-examine life, love and values.

Joanne M. Bargman

That Darn Dane: Hamlet mixes up the orders at his
new bartending job, with hilarious results.

Celebrity Fishing with Ahab: The Cap, Issie and
famous friends go after the big one.

Mr. Noah's Neighbourhood: This week's topic: water
safety. *Normajean McGuire*

The Scarlet Letter: Where Everybody Knows Your
Name. Hester gets a job as a waitress.

The Old Man and the Sea Invitational: This week:
rods, lures and the struggle for the soul.

Nancy L. Clark

Big Brother Inc.: The Corporation tries to maintain
its market share in the face of up-and-coming
independents. *Roberta J. Bergman*

Androcles and the Lion: Andy confronts a thorny
problem.

Life with Count Dracula: Trouble erupts in the
Dracula household when the Count is caught
moonlighting. *Maria J. Bell*

Bonfire of the Vanities: Sherman takes a driving
lesson and learns a new route through the city.

Les Holroyd

Earth, from Space

In honour of Canadian astronaut Roberta Bondar, who was aboard the space shuttle Discovery when it blasted off into space on Jan. 22, 1992, the challenge was to describe Earth from outer space in the style of one of several specified authors.

It was the best of worlds, it was the worst of worlds.
From the rocket, serenity; on the surface,
antagonism. Aloft, seas sparkling and clean; in fact,
cesspools. Above, the forests green and thriving; in
reality, devastated. The Earth, like its human
inhabitants, improves with distance.

Charles Dickens, per K.C. Angus

I see a Planet of Very Little Brain, and all those big
holes in the ozone layer Bother me. "Isn't this
exciting?" I ask Eeyore, as he floats past me.
"No," says Eeyore, banging into a shelf.

A.A. Milne, per Allan Gould

She was sensual, almost spherical, with a land mass that just wouldn't quit, the kind of heavenly body men would kill for. She had all the mountain peaks in all the right places, with more curves than a major-league pitcher. She wore an atmosphere that was so tight it looked like it was held on by gravity, and when she rotated, all eyes were on her and she knew it.

Raymond Chandler, per Brian Yamashita

I'm not going to give you any of that "Gee, it's beautiful" stuff about the Earth. Everybody always says that, and it really bugs me. As if we're supposed to ooh and ah at how profound somebody is for saying so. I can't stand it. I really can't.

J.D. Salinger, per Sheldon Goldfarb

"She's a mother," Holmes replied, "somewhat round at the waist, with an unhealthy constitution in general. She is wearing a tattered blue and green dress, smokes heavily and moves with a singular list to one side."
"Astounding, Holmes," I cried.

Arthur Conan Doyle, per Meredith Andrew

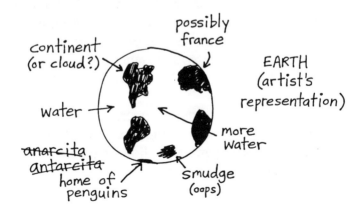

Winnie the Pooh thought that if he looked very hard he could see Piglet's house. So you can imagine his surprise when he heard Piglet's squeaky little voice say, "Hallo Pooh." And then, in an interested sort of way, "What are you doing?"

Well, as it happened, Pooh had collected the right number of honey pots for an expotition of this sort and was once again orbiting Earth.

"I believe, Piglet," said Pooh as he looked down at the funny blue ball that harboured Hundred Acre Wood, "that if you waved your hand very hard I might just be able to see you in your house."

"Silly bear," said the welcomed voice of Christopher Robin. "Piglet's here with me, in Houston."

Pooh didn't know what a houston was or where it might be found, and he wanted to ask Christopher Robin about houstons except his mouth was full of honey owing to a floating honey pot that had bumbled into his lips.

"Say, Pooh," said Christopher Robin in a comforting manner. "That silly old heat shield seems to have separated on take-off. How many honey pots do you have up there?" *A.A. Milne, per Bruce Mohun*

"Planetary, my dear Watson."

Arthur Conan Doyle, per David Fischer

Clerihews

---

*The challenge was to write a clerihew about (a) an
important person, (b) Santa Claus or one of his reindeer,
or (c) an animal. The clerihew is named after its inventor
and champion, E. Clerihew Bentley, whose Biography for
Beginners set the form for the verse: four lines, rhyme
scheme AABB, and the metre doesn't matter, though it
should trip off the tongue when read aloud. The subject's
name is usually in the first line.*

Dr. Norman Bethune
Died in China too soon
And at great expense was resurrected in his
    motherland
As Donald Sutherland.   *David Mayerovitch*

How sharp is Margaret Atwood's pen
In deflating the egos of men;
But consider, boys, ere you beset her:
Her women fare no better.   *John Strebig*

Quick off the mark
Is the wily aardvark.
His goal he will not vary:
First place in the dictionary. *Louise M. Badcock*

Scrooge
Wore rouge
To give him a feeling
He was more appealing. *Tim and Sheila Andrew*

When Aristotle
Turned to the bottle
It was a catastrophe
For Hellenic philosophy.

William Lyon Mackenzie King
Consulted Mama on the littlest thing.
When that vision turned to fog
He relied on his dog.

Queen Elizabeth II
Is married, it's true,
But she still has less fun
Than Elizabeth I. *Tim Andrew*

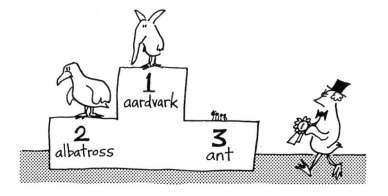

Karl Marx
Was fond of funny little larks,
Like filling the rich with dismay
And leading his housemaid astray.   *R.M. Baxter*

If Malcolm Lowry
Had interests more flowery
He could have potted
And not been besotted.   *Kathy Evans*

Tyrannosaurus Rex
Must have had sex,
Yet no archeologist or miner
Has dug up Tyrannosaurus Regina.
                    Mike Snipper and Lesley P. Lyon

Elizabeth Barrett
Escaped from her garret.
A miraculous cure:
Dad was mad, to be sure.

Acton, Ellis and Currier Bell
Hid their identity quite well
Until fame, all unasked,
The Brontes unmasked.   *Cassie Bradbury*

If Pierre Elliott Trudeau
Had just "given the toe,"
Would the sole of the nation
Have felt agitation?   *Konrad Eisenbichler*

Bill Vander Zalm
Is a natural-born ham.
His grasp of economics
Is the envy of stand-up comics.   *Howard Harris*

An erotic Leonard Cohen song
To the realm of art will always belong.
When Madonna sings of sex
It seems like a reflex.   *Barbara Stowe*

Dylan Thomas
Had an aversion to commas
And read without pauses
The longest clauses.   *Jim Parr*

Sir John A. Macdonald,
When gin was unbottled,
Proposed with impunity
Canada's unity.   *M.L. Anderson*

Barbara Frum, Grand Inquisitor,
Seeks truth from a visitor,
And if answers be not frank
Gives the rack another crank.   *Gertrude E. Gunn*

Dr. Nostradamus
Was no ignoramus.
With nostrums and sutures,
He combined "prophets" and "futures."   *L.E. Jones*

The Reverend Egerton Ryerson
Must have found it extremely tiresome
To make small talk over tea and scones
At Bishop Strachan's.   *Edward Baxter*

Dasher, Dancer, Prancer, Vixen, Comet, Cupid,
    Donner, Blitzen —
The list in a line hardly fits in.
Typically Canadian, Santa Claus
Flouts metric laws.   *Danny Shea*

Rudolph one day
Sought an increase in pay.
Santa gave him a "no"
And the old heave-ho-ho-ho.   *Peter Marucci*

Santa's nightmare gives him the shakes:
Riding along, he loses his brakes.
Rooftopping
Without stopping.   *Leonard Wise*

A tired elf
Said, "Speaking for myself,
A snooze in early December
Would be something to remember."   *Eric Etchen*

Boutros Boutros-Ghali
Is not found in Rand McNally.
He is Secretary-General of the United Nations,
Not a deep gorge in the Carpathians.

Reindeer Comet
For want of a grommet
Broke loose and did dally.
Now orbits like Halley.   *Eric Mendelsohn*

Strange that pursuits Bacchanalian
Are led by a septuagenarian,
Proof that the wiles of St. Nicholas
Ticholas.   *Gordon Findlay*

To the literati Santa brings
Books and other cultural things.
Madonna's creations his elves
Keep for themselves.

Santa, we're told,
Despises the cold.
When he ventures out, cowardly,
He always goes sou'ardly.   *Alanna Little*

Santa or St. Nick,
Take your pick.
Either one
Weighs a ton.   *John Belbeck*

Said Santa, cogitating,
"My act needs updating.
Perhaps the answer
Is a topless Dancer."

J.D. Salinger
Wasn't a Globe challenger,
Preferring to seek the essence
Of adolescence.

The Canadian beaver
Is an underwater achiever.
If you think he's a charmer,
Ask a tree farmer.   *K.C. Angus*

Said the cows and the chickens,
We're scared as the dickens
As to where we'll be at
When they settle the GATT.   *Vi McDowell*

A garden-variety gopher
Would have no use for a chauffeur.
Most, I've found,
Take the underground.   *Betty M. Wolff*

The somnolent cat
Sleeps on the mat
'Cause she has no cushion
To rest her tush on.   *Joan Draper*

The Canadian beaver builds his dam
Without a blueprint diagram
Or ordinances governmental
Concerning things environmental.

A rabbit has a one-track mind:
To eat and reproduce his kind.
The net result of all this fun is
A warren full of little bunnies.   *Arthur M. Lipman*

Brian Mulroney
Invented the loonie,
But because it was eponymous
Chose to remain anonymous.   *S. Sacco*

How wily is the sly raccoon,
He dines at night instead of noon.
That's why his friends are few in number.
He eats our garbage while we slumber.   *June Skene*

In a pinch an armadillo
Can serve as a pillow,
But never recline
On a porcupine.

The camel
Turns up his nose at every other mammal.
He also thinks the Sphinx
Stinks.   *Mike Snipper*

Pity the average cat,
Blissfully unaware that
Malfunctions biological
Could be psychological.   *Adrian Sieunarine*

That unlikely math whiz, the rabbit,
Long ago perfected the habit
Of rapid multiplication
Without a computer work station.   *Gordon Campbell*

The dodo's tale is sad.
He never did anything bad.
One day he just blinked
And woke up extinct.   *I.R. Capewell*

Lonely in Clichéland

In 1992, Britain's Q magazine listed 20 "uniquely lonely figures in clichéland," such as the unpopular hot cake and the work-to-rule beaver. The challenge was to expand on the list.

The cabinet shuffle totally unrelated to the deck chairs on the Titanic.

The team lacking in character that won the championship anyway.

The President who, in the late stages of holding office, acted and walked like a normal, healthy duck.

The bug with the ugly ears, desperately snagged in a deep shag rug.

The person who was given an inch and took only a few feet.

Glen Acorn

A picture worth three words.
The faithful dog who has never once visited his
   master's grave.
A hornless dilemma.
A barrel of miserable monkeys.
A kindly old family doctor who extracted every last
   penny from his impoverished patients.   *Don Suthers*

The swelling violet.
The sloppy pin.
The homely button.
The insomniac log   *Edward Baxter*

The seeing-eye bat.   *Danny Shea*

The animated doornail.   *Cathy Jubenville*

The peacock with low self-esteem.
Guilty women and children.   *Janet Tomkins*

The obstreperous lamb.
The impotent rabbit.
The ingenuous fox.   *A.C. Stone*

The celibate mink.
The cook who spoils the broth while working alone.

Malcolm Westcott

The dog that is man's worst enemy. *Charles Bastomsky*

The unbreakable cookie. *Ann Lotter*

The frazzled cucumber. *Freda Loro*

The absorbent duck. *L.R. de Langley*

The depressed clam.
The malcontent cow. *Karen Newton*

The Cheery Reaper. *Alanna Little*

Environmentally insensitive waters.
An unpopular misconception.
Coming soon to a theatre far from you.
"I was quoted in the proper context."

Sander Schimmelpenninck

A lady of the evening with a heart as hard as a rock.

Charles Crockford

The sensual, fun-loving accountant. *Michael Davies*

A second-best seller. *K.C. Angus*

The thrifty drunken sailor.
The headless chicken with it all together. *Procter LeMare*

Offbeat Job Descriptions

The challenge, devised by Al Wilkinson, was to suggest unusual definitions for job titles. Walter Sowa enclosed a Globe and Mail ad for an "inside parts salesperson" and wondered whether this was a marketer of organ transplants.

Customs officer: advises people on religious and other rituals.

Sound mixer: a reliable bartender. *Morton S. Rapp*

Bank manager: director of river traffic. *Irene Hobsbawn*

Physicist: helper in carbonated-beverage industry.
Gordon Findlay

Disc jockey: chiropractor. *Ed Kamps*

Fortune teller: a bank employee who embezzles.
Live-in nanny: a pet goat. *W. Gordon Kearns*

Veterinarian: someone who helps old soldiers.

André Fillion

Plant supervisor: scarecrow.   *A.F. Powell*

Foreman: precursor to homo sapiens.
Postman: next step in the evolution of homo sapiens.

Paula Archer

Soda jerk: antithesis of the urbane alcoholic.
Window dresser: confirmed exhibitionist.

Robert M. Collins

Shareholder: what Sonny Bono used to be.

Spencer Villam

Pawnbroker: buys and sells partial chess sets.

Daphne Hawkins

Sous-chef: one who cooks for pennies a day.

Brian Yamashita

Locksmith: a hairdresser.   *K.C. Angus*

C&W Shakespeare

Shakespeare's plays have been woefully underused as a source of inspiration for country-and-western songs. I asked for a title or two to repair this omission.

(from *Romeo and Juliet*)
Your Love is Like a Dagger in My Heart
(from *Hamlet*)
These Castle Walls Seem Empty Now
(from *Macbeth*)
I Just Can't Hide (This Stain)   *Jennifer and Jim Duholke*

(from *Macbeth*)
I See Daggers, But All I Grasp is Air   *Anne Anderson*

(from *Merchant of Venice*)
Your Mortgaged Heart
(from *Julius Caesar*)
Run Through Your Man   *Brian Hale*

(from *Antony and Cleopatra*)
My Boyfriend's Back and There's Gonna Be Drama
(from *Henry VIII*)
Freedom's Just Another Word for Annulled,
    Divorced, Beheaded
(from *As You Like It*)
I Would Give What Remains of My Seven Ages For
    You   *Alanna Little*

(from *Romeo and Juliet*)
The Light Through Yonder Window Breaks My
    Heart
(from Rosalind, in *As You Like It*)
I Can't Be Your Woman (If I'm a Better Man Than
    You)   *Ross Murray*

(from *Richard III*)
It's Been a Good Year for the Roses (Dick's Dirge)
                                    Charles Anthony Stuart

(from *Julius Caesar*)
You Stabbed Me on the Senate Steps of Love
(from *Antony and Cleopatra*)
Paralyzed by the Snake Bite of Your Love *Thomas Poldre*

these woods were made for walking.

(from *Richard II*)
When I Was Riding High on Fortune's Wheel
(from *Twelfth Night*)
The Fool Played Viola Like a Fiddle   *Doug Crosbie*

(from *Macbeth*)
Never Shake Thy Gory Locks At Me
(from *Love's Labour's Lost*)
Turning Mortal for Thy Love   *Pamela Snow*

(from *As You Like It*)
All the World's a Stage (And I'm Leaving Town on It
   Tonight)   *J.J. Linden*

(from *Othello*)
Where Is That Hanky That I Gave You?
(from *King Lear*)
I'm Just an Old Man's Fool
(from *Julius Caesar*)
Don't You Leave This House Today   *Eleanor Yeoman*

(from *Romeo and Juliet*)
The Good News Is She Loves Me, The Bad News Is
   She's Gone   *Dale Scaife*

(from *Measure for Measure*)
You Thought You Was a-Lovin' Her, But You Was
   Lovin' Me
(from *Hamlet*)
Momma, Don't Kiss Uncle No More   *M.J. Williams*

(from *Macbeth*)
These Woods Were Made for Walking
          Michael and Nancy Parke-Taylor

(from *Romeo and Juliet*)
Let's Love Each Other to Death
(from *Two Gentlemen of Verona*)
How Was I to Know He Would Be My Gal?   *Earl Liu*

(from *Midsummer Night's Dream*)
What Honky-Tonk Angel Wakes Me From My
    Flower Bed?
(from *Merchant of Venice*)
The Quality of Mercy Is Not Strain'd (Into This
    Whisky I'm Drinking to Kill My Pain)   *Rick Rathwell*

(from *The Tempest*)
I Was Driftin' on a Stormy Sea Till I Landed on the
    Shores of Your Love
(from *Romeo and Juliet*)
Your Love Is Like a Poison I Swallowed By Mistake
    Robin Breon

(from *Merchant of Venice*)
I Really Don't Want a Pound of Flesh Unless The
    Flesh Is Yours
(from *The Tempest*)
Many Things Are Washed Up in a Storm, And Now
    What's Washed Up Is Us   *Charles Crockford*

Modern Maxims

The world is blessed with any number of old maxims: A stitch in time saves nine; there's no fool like an old fool. The challenge was to devise a new, modern maxim: A Walkman is only as good as its tape; it's a limber soul who survives aerobics class. If a few of these don't enter the language, there's no justice.

Today's Ninja Turtle is tomorrow's ET.
The smaller the portions, the costlier the meal.
Taping doesn't guarantee watching.
Even the smallest Kleenex forgotten leaves lint on the
    laundry. *Carolyn Vose and Alan Davis*

Feed the Blue Box, starve the dump.
No rose as fair as the roof that retracts. *Kay Dills*

The capacity of the subway car is equal to the number
    of people who want to get on. *James Asplin*

The squeaky wheel gets the axe. *F.M. Grossman*

The early bird gets the parking space.
Be nice to the people you meet on the way up, in case
the elevator gets stuck.
Don't blight the land that feeds you.
If at first you don't succeed, try for a government
grant. *Al Wilkinson*

When the going gets tough, the tough amend their
array of policy options. *Will Chabun*

A watched microwave never beeps.
You can't tell a book by its author's frequent
appearances on TV to flog it.
The proof of the pudding is in the list of chemical
ingredients. *Hank Dayton*

If you put a tin plate in a microwave, don't be
surprised when the sparks fly. *Tony Rother*

Politics is stranger than fiction.
A watched stoplight never changes. *Charles Crockford*

You're only as desperate as the people who write the
companions-wanted ads you read. *Holly McPhee*

beware of stockbrokers bearing advice.

A penny saved is a waste of time.
An ounce of Spandex covers a pound of her. *Les Holroyd*

Out of telecommunications, out of touch with life.
Plastic surgery makes perfect.
There's more to a newspaper than meets the eye.
Trust a politician until he is elected. *Rob McMenemy*

Waste is a terrible thing to mind. *Janet Collins*

The faster we circumnavigate the globe, the slower
we commute to work. *Carolyn Beck*

Better a good cook in an untidy kitchen than designer
glitz on the menu.
Beware of stockbrokers bearing advice.
It is easier for a camel to pass through the eye of a
needle than for an intelligent adult to program a
VCR.
Designer jeans must still be washed. *Arthur M. Lipman*

A fool and his money receive a warm welcome at a
pub party.
The bigger they are, the more likely you'll share your
train seat with their parcels.
What's sauce for the goose is sure to contain deadly
levels of cholesterol.
Pride goeth before the fitting-room mirrors.
Alanna Little

Better a safe than sorry. *Michael Kerman*

Biblical
Headlines

The challenge, courtesy of Doug Brown, was to devise a Biblical headline. I learned a few things in judging this one, including what the Gadarene pigs were all about (Luke 8:32-33). I hope most of these names are generally known, even to people not raised with the Old and / or New Testament as their holy book, but I can tell you that I consulted the library's Biblical concordance more than once. When in doubt, go thou and do likewise.

Pork futures soar in wake of Gadarene calamity.

L. Chichoco

Dietitians claim loaves and fishes not a balanced
    meal. *Cherry Watson*

Man smites Og: Bashan king dies in battle with
    Israelites. *Shoel Silver*

Mole suspected in Apostle supper club.
Salt futures dive on news of Lot's wife. *Ian D. Brown*

Rains to stop soon, says government meteorologist;
  Noah's prediction 'pure hokum.'
Success reported in fusion experiment: 'Let there be
  light,' says device's creator.
Liquor licencing board to investigate 'water into
  wine' at wedding; may be subject to tax, says
  procurator. *Eric Mendelsohn*

Red Sea parted, bridge plans on hold. *Don Smith*

God confirms change to six-day work week.
More troubles at Tower, management says union
  'doesn't speak our language.' *Simon Elliott Parker*

'Let there be light' decree boosts sun-block stocks.
Innovative rib surgery ensures gender balance.
Pharaoh slams Deity's 'pro-Israelite bias' as threat to
  Mideast peace process. *David Mayerovitch*

Man brought back to life sues village healer: 'I was
   better off dead.'
Couple held on charges of larceny and trespass;
   husband blames wife, wife claims family pet told
   her to.   *Joe Keogh*

Galilean council initiates pollution probe after man
   walks on water.
King Nebuchadnezzar sues furnace-maker after three
   survive.   *Trevor J. Harvey*

Absalom not wearing protective headgear at time of
   riding accident, coroner rules.   *G.A. Corcoran*

Rescued sheep protests, 'I wasn't lost!'
No plants registered for voyage; Noah confronts
   Green Party.   *David G. Smith*

Scientists examine unusual sodium deposit in desert.
                                           Helen McCusker

Get haircut or go: Delilah issues ultimatum.
Moses demand refused; adultery still in.
David-Bathsheba love talk taped by Mossad.
Pregnant mom finds no room at inn; welfare officials
   acknowledge housing problem.
Lazarus says tomb now surplus.   *David E. Bawden*

Unusual same-sex stalking charges laid by Naomi
   against Ruth   *Margaret Higgins*

Local prophet before human-rights tribunal, hires
   male disciples only.   *John Kooistra*

Methusaleh dead at 969; sprightly patriarch attributed
longevity to regular begetting. *Ken Purvis*

Animal-rights activists demand end to testing of
demons on pigs. *Alfreda Skenfield*

Job outlook dismal. *Irene Hobsbawn*

God creates heavens; Earth still awaiting permit.
Weather outlook: partly cloudy for next 40 days,
nights.
Man blinded in freak highway accident near
Damascus. *Jane Wangersky*

Four horsemen heading for showdown, psychic
predicts.
Proposed environmental assessment delays Moses'
sea crossing. *Nick Vandervoort*

Good-time girl was enemy agent, Jericho survivor
charges.
Grieving family urges ban on slings for minors.
R.M. Baxter

See Page 4 for revised Red Sea tide tables.
One-quarter of world's population wiped out in
senseless killing of brother.
Mess of pottage scam uncovered. *Arthur M. Lipman*

Jonah swears off seafood: the inside story.
Manna falls from heaven again; travellers bemoan
monotony of diet. *William M. Vance*

Ousted Adam and Eve predict population explosion.
Ark to fly flag of convenience.   *Edward W. Barrett*

Jericho building inspector faces corruption charges.
Thomas casts doubt on reincarnation theory.
                                          Al Wilkinson

Correction: Lazarus obituary.   *Chris Hurst*

Israel announces free trade with Canaan: eye for eye,
    tooth for tooth; opponents claim deal will cause
    pain and suffering.   *Christian Schumann*

Camel stuck in eye of needle in bizarre religious ritual.
                                          Doug Brown

Clothing giants eye untapped Eden market.   *Phil Gurski*

Ten new laws written in stone; no amending formula,
    says Moses.   *Hilary Ostrov*

David 1, Giants 0.   *Anita Arnold*

Fish lands man.   *John Sullivan*

Wine was watery, say Cana wedding guests.
Witness claims Lazarus was only holding his breath.
                                          H. Hargreaves

Philistines demand David be tested for steroids.
Hairdresser Delilah has licence lifted.
Money-changers demand better security.   *B. Moore*

Judge orders ban on publication of evidence in case of
Susannah v. Elders.   *Marian Cullen*

Who turned on the lights? Creation enters second day.
                                              Joe Sinko

Noah still dubious; plans Ark II.   *Jim Parr*

Gabriel Courier Co. delivers news of miracle baby to
childless couple.
Eden Apple Co. opens 'pick your own' orchard.
Ark offers family mystery cruises.
Burning bush; arson suspected.
                          Elizabeth Buckmaster and Will Easton

Human-rights commission charges Pearly Gates
operator with discrimination.   *Glenda Bocknek*

Ezekiel held for psychiatric examination.
Police not releasing name of young offender in
'Goliath' slaying.   *R.G. MacNeill*

Flood damage exceeds initial estimates.
Sodom, Gomorrah see record temperatures.
Abraham's nanny leaves after 'sand upon seashore'
announcement.   *John Belbeck*

Lost Positives

The challenge, suggested by James K. Mann, was to supply lost positives. Philip Currah found this line in P.G. Wodehouse's 1938 book The Code of the Woosters: "He spoke with a certain what-is-it in his voice, and I could see that, if not actually disgruntled, he was far from being gruntled."

And Art Phillips wrote, a few weeks after the contest: "Normally, I am an ept, ert and reasonably dolent person, so I don't know how I missed your column on such an occuous subject as lost positives. I can't blame my kids. They were so ruly that they were actually a traction. I wanted to write to apologize and to ask why a flammable object is inflammable, and could ique (as in unique) be a synonym for common?"

A gatecrasher is a vited guest.   *Steve Paulsson*

Fantile: Adult, mature.
Mense: Tiny.
Bibed: Refrained from drinking.   *Al Wilkinson*

Stemious: Given to liberal consumption of booze.
    Keith Ketchen

Ciple: A leader. *K.C. Nolan*

Posable: Environmentally friendly. *Stephen Maude*

If discussing the Constitution leads nowhere, cussing
it must be very productive. *Karl Dilcher*

If a mishap is an unfortunate accident, is a hap a
fortunate one? *John deVisser*

An appointing Christmas exceeds expectations.
Jean O'Grady

Is a creet person a blabbermouth?
Is the taff side the male side? *Jackie Van't Hullenaar*

Combobulate: To put in order. *Jane Wangersky*

Parage: To praise. *Pat Johnson*

Jected: Flying high. *Doris Richards*

Tort: Twist into shape. *Barry Wever*

A missed employee must keep his or her job.

A.S. Zakrzewski

Sident: One who agrees with establishment policy.
Communicado: Carrying a portable telephone.

J.J. Linden

Solent: Polite, humble.
Traught: Serene.
Bilitated: Strengthened.
Praved: Ethical.

Marguerite Frost

Dissolving ice is messier than solving water.

Marvin Schwartz

Iquitous: Righteous.

Lee Tokar

A tant object must be near at hand.

Sev Heiberg

Cellaneous: Homogeneous.

Simon Warder

Dies (origin, derwear): Overclothes.

Roz Paris

Co describes music that is not inane, that doesn't
have a strong beat and that you can't dance to.

Brian Yamashita

Bauch: To instill morality and celibacy.

Russell Yapp

Broglio: A clear, uncomplicated situation.

Jack Orbaum

If by immolating something we set it afire, do we
douse it by molating it?

John and Gail Benjafield

Sult: To speak nicely to someone.
Fant: An old person.
Struction: The process of removing knowledge from
   an individual.
Semble: To be absolutely honest and straightforward.
Quisitive: Totally lacking in curiosity.
Plussed: Understanding what is happening.

Tim and Sheila Andrew

Aster: Sudden or great good fortune. *Philip Currah*

A tinguished citizen is seldom invited to dine with
   royalty.
A tracted observer has great powers of concentration.
Is a cussion a brooding silence?
Misers insist on tributing their wealth.
I want to live in a neighbourhood where there is a
   turbance every night. *Jim Reynolds*

It was early in the evening, and the crowd was
   starting to perse. *Les Holroyd*

Feit money is genuine.
If a lackadaisical person is irresponsible, an adaisical
   person can be counted on. *Helen Bagshaw*

I'm not mistaken, I'm taken. *Judy Cornwell*

Pensable: Essential. *Roger Cullman*

If a misanthrope hates humankind, an anthrope must
   love everyone. *Paul and Margaret Lewis*

Written for Children

The challenge was to devise names of children's books that might have been written by famous authors. This one was suggested by Joe Keogh, who credited Dave Sadkin of Niagara University's English Department for the idea. The response was greater than usual, and there were the predictable number of multiple responses: Hemingway's The Old Man and the ABC, Shakespeare's Green Eggs and Hamlet, Dickens' A Tale of Two Kitties and Margaret Mitchell's Gone With the Wind in the Willows.

Charles Dickens: Dumbo and Son
Franz Kafka: The Castle Mystery
John Le Carré: A Small Toy in Germany
Machiavelli: The Prince and the Pea   *Graham Johnson*

Aldous Huxley: Pointing is Not Polite   *Shelley Gaffe*

William Faulkner: Get Down Off That Chair,
Absalom!
Boris Pasternak: The Visit to Doctor Zhivago

Donald McGrath

Oscar Wilde: The Importance of Being Ernie and Bert
Ernest Hemingway: To Have and to Not Be Allowed
to Have *Doug Lalonde*

Tennessee Williams: The Cat in the Hat on a Hot Tin
Roof
Thomas Wolfe: Lassie, You Can Go Home Again

Wayne Cunningham

Robert Louis Stevenson: Dr. Jekyll and Mr.
Hide-and-Go-Seek *Nigel Yonge*

Ian Fleming: Goldfinger Painting *Geoff Williams*

Hardy: Far From the Muddy Crowd *Henrietta Johnson*

Steinbeck: The Grapes of Raffi *Brian Halpin*

Hemingway: The Old Man and the Seesaw
Tolstoy: War and Peekaboo
James Joyce: Finnegans Wakey-Wakey
Edgar Allan Poe: The Pit and the Pablum
Joseph Heller: Catch 22, Buckle Your Shoe
Dostoevsky: Notes from the Playground   *Glenda Bocknek*

Amy Tan: The Toy Duck Club   *Audrey M. Bates*

Harper Lee: It's Not Nice to Kill a Mockingbird
Andrea Douglas

Le Carré: The Boy Who Came Home With a Cold
Nathaniel Hawthorne: The House with the Seven
   Gerbils
Nevil Shute: At the Beach   *John Adlington*

E.M. Forster: Howard's Beginning: Preparing for
   Your New Brother   *Jim Parr*

Michael Ondaatje: In the Skin of the Lion, the Witch
   and the Wardrobe
Tom Clancy: The Hunt for Red Riding Hood
Linda Lumsden

Arthur Miller: The Sad Tale of a Grumpy Salesman
Ruth Brown

Le Carré: The Honourable Schoolboy Always Does
   His Homework
Jerome K. Jerome: Three Men in a Boat Should
   Wear Life Jackets   *Angela Colm*

Elizabeth Smart: In the Kindergarten I Sat Down and
Played   *Lesley Christie*

Douglas Coupland: No-Tears-Shampoo Planet
Stephen Hawking: A Brief History of Bedtime
                                                   Sarah Grasset

Edward Albee: Who's Afraid of Woof Woof?
                                                   Lisa Shapiro

Madonna: Six!   *William G. Alexander*

D.H. Lawrence: The Virgin, the Gypsy and the
Candlestick-Maker   *Dwayne Moholitny*

Salman Rushdie: A Devil's Garden of Verses
                                                   Martin Julien

H.G. Wells: Connect-the-Dots Outline of History
Machiavelli: The Prince's Pop-up Activity Book
                                                   Rick Lymer

Le Carré: The Spy Who Came In When He Was Told
Truman Capote: This Little Piggie Had Breakfast at
Tiffany's   *Maria J. Bell*

F. Scott Fitzgerald: Tender is the Nightlight
                                                   Carole Vaughan

Roget's Tyrannosaurus
Chaucer: Can't Be Telling Tales
Dostoevsky: War on Peas   *Hubert M. Butcher*

Erica Jong: Fear of Lying   *Neil Dring*

Ernest Buckler: The Mountain and the Valley: A First
Book of Opposites   *Helen McCusker*

Shakespeare: The Tying of the Shoe   *Daylene Podmore*

Play-Doh's Republic   *Mark Wilson*

Wells: The Little Time Machine That Could
Poe: The House of Usha, Usha, We All Fall Down
                    English department of Elmwood School

Marcel Proust: A la Recherche de Waldo
Alexandre Dumas: Monte Cristo's First Book of
Numbers   *M. Moorfield*

Tom Wolfe: The Right and Left Stuff   *Shawn McSweeny*

Hemingway: The Sun Also Has to Go to Bed   *Joe Keogh*

Agatha Christie: Let's Pretend We're Murdered on
the Orient Express
Heller: 22 Ways to Play Catch
Karl Marx: Das Kapital Letters
T.S. Eliot: The Wind in the Waste Land   *Heather Peacock*

Orwell: 1,984 Things to Do on a Rainy Day
Bram Stoker: My Two New Teeth   *Michael Peacock*

Lawrence: Lady Chatterley's Special Friend
                                        Susan Dance

Wells: The How to Tell Time Machine   *Phil Gurski*

Sophocles: Oedipus 'n' Boots   *John Bishopric*

Shakespeare: Henry is 5!   *Elisheva Lightstone*

Virginia Woolf: How to Look After a Room of One's
   Own   *Patrisha Robertson*

Shakespeare: Henry II II and the Hooded Fang
Pearl Buck: Good Earth, Bad People: A Young
   Person's Guide to Streetproofing   *Zal Yanovsky*

Evelyn Waugh: Scoop, the Naughty Puppy   *Fred Farr*

Alice Walker: The Purple Colouring Book
Thoreau: Where's Walden?
Agatha Christie: Horton Hears a Whodunnit
Dumas: The Man in the Halloween Mask
W.O. Mitchell: Who Broke the Wind?
                              Julia Phillips and Peter Shore

Mary Shelley: Let's Play Doctor
Shakespeare: Much Ado About Bedtime
Homer: Are We There Yet? Odysseus Takes a Trip
Orwell: Big Brother is Teasing Me   *Alanna Little*

William Blake: Sing-Songs of Experience   *John Belbeck*

Plus a Letter

The challenge was to insert an extra letter into a sentence to comic effect. This was suggested by K.C. Angus, whose example was: In 1862, John Speke discovered the head waiters of the Nile.

If you drink, don't drivel.   *George E. Jackson*

The wealthy passenger always carried a heavy purser
    over his shoulder.
The wounded called Florence Nightingale "the lady
    with the clamp."
By computer networking he discovered his family
    robots.
The source of the explosion was a faulty meteor.
                                          Jim Parr

The ministers approved the bill with just a few
    altercations.
With the increased mill rate, property owners faced
    startling reality taxes.
The PM commended the senator for his loyalty and
    trough-mindedness.   *Alanna Little*

Eating caviar is hazardous to your health, according
to the sturgeon-general. *Peter Marucci*

If you seek justice, you'll find the flaw is not always
on your side. *Percy Junger*

A long, tedious speech was given by the executive
voice-president.
In summer, the beaches are crowded moistly with
children.
If we can send a man to the moon, why can't we find
a curse for the common cold? *Maria Bell*

And so the world and everything in it was saved
because of Noah's little lark.
Animal-rights activists object to the use of brats in
medical research. *Fred Farr*

He was a philanthropist and a great supporter of the
tarts. *Linda Lumsden*

The North American free-tirade agreement should be
ratified in 1993. *Claire Molson*

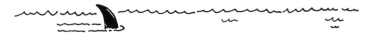

"shark!" the herald angels sing.

An old-fashioned quill pen makes a delightful and
appropriate gift for Feather's Day.   *Mary Dando*

Remember the days of scareless love?   *David Dunsmuir*

The game between the Cardinals and the Blue Jays
was stopped for 10 minutes when a flight broke out.
He keeps his instructions in a learn-to behind his
house.   *Charles Crockford*

Don't tell me how to ruin my business!
The Buick stops here.
I can't write poetry any more; my mouse has left me.
Always keep your tempter under control.
On our last trip to Italy I fell in love with Florence,
but my wife couldn't tear herself away from
Romeo.   *Edward Baxter*

A fool and his money are soon partied.
Beware the ideas of March.   *Glenda Bocknek*

The minister announced that a substantial slum will
be allocated to public housing.   *Al Wilkinson*

Professor Jones was invited to present a pauper on
economics.   *Dorothy M. Poole*

Thirsty days hath September, April, June and
November.
Education is the best provision for old rage.   *Don Suthers*

Biology 101 offers two lectures, plus one lamb
experiment a week.   *D. Kenny*

Man is a noble salvage.
I take my fund where I find it.   *Helen McCusker*

This time, when leaving the hotel he remembered to
  trip the doorman.   *Doug Broderick*

The veteran heavyweight showed the fans that he still
  packs an impressive paunch.   *Peter Wildeblood*

M. Richler's writings are mostly works of light
  friction.
When the missionary tried to drive Sadie Thompson
  out of business he received a prude awakening.
The sons shared a strong family resemblance; they all
  looked a lout like their father.   *A. Taylor*

For added protection on his long voyage, he asked
  the nurse to give him some extra shorts.
With little or no education, few English pheasants
  were able to read or write.   *Ken Purvis*

The doctor's invention proved worthless since he
  couldn't obtain a patient.
Some folks just sweep their worries under the drug.
                                            E. Warren Steiner

He will give the devil his duel.
This was the unkindest cult of all.   *David Savage*

"Shark!" the herald angels sing.   *Deanna Silverman*

Last Words of Animals

The challenge, borrowed from Britain's New Statesman, was to transcribe the last words of animals, famous or otherwise.

The Road Runner, hooked up to a life-support
   system: "Beep Beep Beeeep...."   *Jennifer Kuta*

Camel: "Careful with that straw!"   *Phil Gurski*

Alligator: "See you later, man."   *Helen McCusker*

Sheep: "Nurse, please pull the wool over my eyes."
     David Savage

Lemming: "Of course I'm over the hill. We're all over the hill."

Bear: "Happy third birthday, Davy Crockett."

Parrot: "Hi, I'm here to audition for the Monty Python show."

Slug: "Thanks, waiter, I'll just have a beer and pretzels."   *Alanna Little*

Hyena: "Ha ha ha ha ow ow ow ow ha ha ha ha."
Jennifer Markowitz

Felix the Cat: "It's the end of the ninth."

Swan: "They're playing my song."   *Yvonne Robinson*

The owl and the pussycat: "Life preservers are so unromantic."   *Cherry and Alan Watson*

Queen bee: "What do you mean, you're going on strike?"   *Linda Lumsden*

Cock Robin: "What's that whistling sound?"

Donald Duck: "You're having *what* à l'orange?"
Peter Marucci

wait a minute -- i paid for a round trip.

lemmings

Penguin: "Goodbye, cool world."   *Martin Goldstein*

Moose: "Of course this shortcut is safe. Just stay
   between the steel rails."
Ant: "Come see this funny-looking animal with the
   long snout."
Hamelin rat: "I love a parade."   *Al Wilkinson*

Eeyore: "I knew this would happen."
                    Peter Hood-Morris and students

The RCA Victor dog: "At my funeral, please — no
   music."   *Charles Crockford*

"Huff and puff...? And then what did he say?"
Diplodocus: "Asteroi...!"
Turkey: "Come on, let's join the settlers. They're
   giving thanks or something."
"Cow network news, Bossie reporting. Well, the trip
   was bumpy and crowded, but we got here. Now
   we're all just standing around. Oh, oh, something's
   happening in the line just ahead of me."
"Okay, okay. Not to panic. I am Dr. Schroedinger's
   cat. I am Dr. Schroedinger's cat."
"C'mon, Mom! I'm just hanging around with all the
   other fish waiting for the new pulp mill to start up."
                    Graham Hagens

Clam: "Is this a digger I see before me?"
                    Wayne Cunningham

Postal Poems

The challenge was to write a poem in the style of any poet, on the theme of the post office or fax machine, in six lines or fewer. S.F. Sommerfeld tried a longer one for fun (in the style of A.E. Housman) and I've included it here.

Mary had a little stamp,
She stuck it on a letter.
On second thought she steamed it off,
Deciding fax was better.
Allen B. Gibb

I've never seen a fax machine, I hope I never will.
I'm happy with my crystal set, I'm happy with my
    quill.
I much prefer the spoken word, the letter penned by
    hand.
Why people call me "dinosaur" I'll never understand.
Lesley P. Lyon

As extinct as the bronto
Is mail service pronto.
K.C. Angus

I sent a letter to my love.
Alas! The mailman lost it.
It turned up in another bag
Where inside workers tossed it.
My love, she died. Eventually
The letter was returned to me.

Anne Spencer

When stamps were one and twenty,
I heard the postmen say:
"We promise prompt delivery
Today and every day —
Affix the proper postage,
Please use the postal code,
It's only one and twenty
To anyone's abode."
When stamps were one and twenty
I heard them say again:
"We've got to raise the postage —
Please bear the short-term pain.
We'll be much more efficient,
The better to serve you."
Now stamps are three and forty,
And oh, not true, not true.

S.F. Sommerfeld

Double Dactyls

The challenge was to write a double dactyl, an eight-line verse whose fourth and eighth lines rhyme. The metre is DA da da DA da da in all lines but the fourth and eighth, where it is DA da da DA. Strictly speaking, one of the lines should be a single word, though I didn't make that a condition. As you will see, a couple of people expressed (mock?) exasperation with the choice of Challenge. The "Presto" referred to is Reform Party leader Preston Manning.

Andrew Macpherson offered a helpful footnote to his verse about Vilhjalmur Stefansson: "Stefansson was born in Manitoba in 1879 and explored the western and high Arctic between 1906 and 1918. Of dubious reputation in Canada, not entirely deservedly, he passed most of his life in the United States, where he died in 1962. He was an opinionated food faddist, abhorring salt as much as tobacco, and championing the eating of fat. (One of his many books was Not By Bread Alone.)"

Higgledy piggledy
Mickey and Minnie Mouse
Lovers on celluloid
Partners in fun.
Live now at Disneyland
Welcoming visitors
Selling themselves (say cheese!),
Trapped in the sun.

Higgledy piggledy
Ignorant Icarus
Trying his wings so new
Soared in the sky.
Daedalus warned his boy,
"Don't go too near the sun!"
Typical teen-ager
Never asked why.

Glenda Bocknek

...trapped in the sun

Higgledy piggledy
George Bush the President
Fought in the desert with
Saddam Hussein.
Then when his ratings were
Too low for comfort he
Had to go back there and
Do it again.

Bartley Bard

Higgledy piggledy
Sherlock of Baker Street
Based his deductions on
What Watson said.
Holmes from experience
Knew that if Watson thought
A was the criminal,
B was instead.

Higgledy piggledy
Arthur Duke Wellington
Conquered Napoleon
Caused him to flee.
Bonaparte afterwards
Claimed that his hemorrhoids
Plagued and distracted him.
Sore loser he.

Higgledy piggledy
Juliet Capulet
Fell for a Montague
Hoping to wed.
After a duel and a
Tryst on a balcony
Weird machinations left
Both of them dead.

K.C. Angus

Higgledy piggledy
Gilbert and Sullivan
Wrote *The Mikado* with
Schoolgirl Yum Yum.
Now for the life of me
I can't stop warbling,
"Rum titty, rum titty,
Rum titty tum."

Margaret Whitelegg

Higgledy piggledy
Presto's a giggle, de-
Termined to wriggle, de-
Nying his views;
He's got the nerve to give
Policies swervative:
Ultraconservative
Nightmares come true.

David Ingham

Higgledy piggledy
Gaius Caligula
Ever-incestually
Seeking true bliss:
Hypermendaciously
Spurned by his mother, he
Overfraternally
Turned to his sis.

Dirk L. Shaeffer

Higgledy piggledy,
Anna McGarrigle
Sings with her sister and
Does it first-rate.
Apologetically
I must inquire, though:
Which one is Anna and
Which one is Kate?

Eric Mendelsohn

Higgledy piggledy
Ludwig van Beethoven
Opted for song more than
Women and wine.
Then he grew weary of
All that was metrical.
That's why there isn't a
Tenth. He said, "Nein."

Higgledy piggledy
Judas Iscariot
Won't be forgiven his
Sins — few were worse.
When they reproached him, he
Said, "That's all true, but my
Name has the metre for
Dactylic verse."   *Jim Parr*

Higgledy piggledy
Vilhjalmur Stefansson
Sledged on the Arctic seas
Living on seals.
Always, reportedly,
Though not monastic he
Eschewed tobacco and
Salt with his meals.   *Andrew Macpherson*

Higgledy piggledy
Pablo Picasso, he
Scribbled and painted and
Drew what he saw.
How he was able to
Filter reality
Making it art simply
Fills me with awe.   *Karen Pratte*

Higgledy piggledy
Good Queen Elizabeth
England's first feminist
Kept her slate clean.
Financed her admirals'
Rampaging voyages
Earning the title of
Voyagin' Queen.

Mike Snipper

Higgledy piggledy
Willie Mackenzie King
Spent his declining year
Flirting with spooks,
Constantly swayed by mere
Phantasmagoria.
Maybe Mulroney, too?
That's how it looks.

David Dunsmuir

Higgledy piggledy
Challenge in Globe and Mail
Often is comical,
This one's a dud.
"DA da da DA da da,"
Dactyls are hard as hell
And the instructions were
As clear as mud.

Bradley Crawford

Higgledy piggledy
Globe and Mail newspaper
Made up some challenge that
Readers could try.
Foremost the stupidest:
Dactyls in double, yet
Here am I trying, so
Stupidest, I.

Jo S. Meingarten

Abrupt Endings

The challenge was to devise a line that would bring an abrupt, premature end to a book, play or movie. The idea came from Globe colleague Joan Danard, who offered her own candidate: "Hello, Godot." I responded with: "On the first day, God rested." Then everyone got into the act.

(from *Moby Dick*)
Call me fishmeal.

And Pilate said: "In view of the pre-sentence report, I have no alternative but to reduce the sentence from crucifixion to two years probation. Next case."

Eric Mendelsohn

(from *The Old Man and the Sea*)
"@#$%!! The line broke!"

Boy Staunton's snowball hit me right smack on the backside, the rock producing a welt of fire.

David Zielenko

(from *Field of Dreams*)
"I think it said, 'If you grill it, I'll have some.'"
(from *Rosemary's Baby*)
"Rosemary darling, this is Dr. Morgentaler, simply
    the best in town."
(from *E.T.*)
"How was I supposed to know it would have a fatal
    allergy to Reese's Pieces?"   *Donald Yapp*

Hamlet: "Mom, I think it's great that you and Uncle
    Claudius got hitched."   *Fred, Rachel and Victoria Yehia*

"It's Christmas Day, Cratchit, and I suddenly feel
    good about myself. Take the rest of the day off and
    use this money to buy a turkey."   *Glen Acorn*

"Tempting, Pickering, but I never make a wager."
                                                Philippa Hunter

"Not now, Lady Chatterley, I have to feed the
    pheasants."   *Dave Nickerson*

Hansel: "No way, I'm allergic to gingerbread."
Welcome to the Inn: Vacancy.   *H. Metszies*

Cordelia: "I too love you, father, with all my heart,
more than words can say." *John Rowell*

"Androcles ... It's not the same lion!"
So Little Red Riding Hood decided to stay home and
watch Coronation Street instead of visiting her
grandmother.
Oedipus: "Mother, how wonderful to see you again
after all these years. I would have recognized you
anywhere." *Frank Haigh*

I knew I could turn this hideaway into an ideal tourist
spot, and soon Walden Trailer Park was a reality.
Alanna Little

(from *Romeo and Juliet*)
"The termites have struck again! That balcony will
have to go!"
(from *Rebel Without a Cause*)
"You're so right, Dad." *Audrey M. Bates*

Eve to Adam: "I think I'll have my tubes tied."
The Peters family

John Galsworthy's The Forsyte Haiku. *Linda Lumsden*

It is an ancient mariner, and he stoppeth nobody.
Elizabeth Quance

(from *Kramer vs Kramer*)
"Fine, leave me, and take that runny-nosed kid with
you." *Carole Vaughan*

"Okay, we'll do it your way, Mr. Christian."
"Mmmm. Seconds! Thank you, Mr. Bumble."
"But Desdemona uses Kleenex!"   *Barbara S. Wanless*

"The zoning bylaw requires bricks, Mr. Pig.
                              Mary McClelland

"Arthur, a square table will suit the room better."
"Sorry, Achilles, you didn't pass the army medical."
"Big Brother doesn't care what you do."   *Neil Packham*

Cinderella's widowed father never remarried.
                              Irene M. Nickerson

The animals entered the ark, one by one.
'Twas the night after Christmas.   *Tony Carroll*

(from *Pride and Prejudice*)
It is a truth universally acknowledged, that a single
    man in possession of a good fortune must be in
    want of a stockbroker.   *Robert Nielsen*

(from *Through the Looking Glass*)
The mirror shattered.   *S. Denyer*

"I'm sorry, Miss Poppins, the position has been
    filled."   *Jim Packham*

"Among the items destroyed in the fire was a recently
    completed portrait of dashing socialite Dorian
    Gray."   *Christopher Busby*

Index of Contributors